WRITE
A NEW
SONG

WRITE A NEW SONG

Discovering the Hidden
Songwriting Skills Inside of You

Mateo Blae

OTHER
HERO

First published 2021 by Other Hero Books

ISBN 978-1-7399158-1-0 HB
ISBN 978-1-7399158-0-3 TPB

 @MateoBlae

mateoblae.com

Sing to the Lord a new song;
sing to the Lord, all the earth.

Psalms 96:1

CONTENTS

CAN YOU BE A SONGWRITER?

"Words make you think a thought.
Music makes you feel a feeling.
A song makes you feel a thought."

—Yip Harburg

That's an important question to ask.

What if you *could* be a songwriter? Should you? Would it be okay for you to write a song that matters to *you* – and maybe to others as well?

A true songwriter takes a piece of his or her soul in hand, transferring it to a pen or pencil, then starts writing out that piece of his or her soul on paper where it becomes its own existence. Its own thriving voice that came from *you* – one that deserves to be heard by many.

In the end, if you don't have the passion and drive to go beyond just writing a song because you want to see how it works, or see if you're good at it, or just want to experiment, understand that you may not experience the same joy and accomplishment in creating something worthwhile without the goal of becoming what you've always wanted to be: a songwriter.

So ask yourself that important question: do you *want* to be a songwriter, and why?

It's not easy. No one ever said it was.

Writing songs has always been therapeutic in nature. After all, it's like poetry. When you express yourself, you're shedding skin. In its place will be new skin to protect yourself from the elements. Because it's therapeutic, you'll hold those creations close to your heart for good reason. But here's the catch:

Songs were meant to be sung. *That* means you're inviting listeners to really *hear* who you are.

Ask yourself: are you ready for that?

You are. You need only to give yourself 'permission' to open yourself up to the idea. The drive and creativity sleep inside you. All you need to do is break the locks.

Songs are *meant* to be performed. Not one single song in history was written solely for reading. That would be silly. If it's meant to be a song, it's meant to jump off the paper and into someone's voice or instrument – whether that be your voice or someone else's is the question. In the end, that doesn't matter.

Because *you* know that those words belong to you, and it can be frightening to hear your own heart sing on a record. Might even be all the more frightening to sing on stage a song *you*, yourself, wrote. But rest assured: it may be scary, but it's all the more liberating, and empowering.

The challenge many have in trying to conquer the fear of songwriting (and consequently singing in general) is that you might have that doubt in your head that you won't be any good at it. Understand this:

- If you have *any* musical talent with an instrument, you most definitely *are* a songwriter

- If you like music, you can most definitely be a songwriter
- If you can even hum a tune at a decent pitch... you're definitely of songwriter material

What you have to realize is that it's not about whether or not you can do it, but if you really *want* to. There are many stressors in songwriting:

- *What am I thinking? I'm not going to be good at it!*
- *Too competitive*
- *Emotionally stressful*
- *I'm not in a 'good place' to focus on this*

Never mind the intimidating idea of exposing your feelings. That alone could potentially be earth-shattering to the soul. So *please* do understand: it's important to *want* this, and if you do, don't ever be afraid of being what you want to be. *Allow* yourself to be what you dream.

Forget the setbacks, the stories, the fear, the worries.

Don't fret. Don't fear. Your story isn't alone. The greats of the music industry stand with you, and you never know what may come of it until you put all your passion behind it.

What you're going to experience here in this book is simple: you'll access everything you need to accomplish the dream of becoming the songwriter you've always wanted to be. We'll cover areas such as:

- The right mindset to boost creativity
- True confidence in soulful songwriting
- The right tools to craft creative and original content
- Basic music knowledge for sexy syncopation and synchronization

- And more strategies for collaboration

My name is Mateo Blae, singer, songwriter, producer, and arranger. I've had the opportunity to write, copyright, and record countless songs with the strategies and methodologies listed in this book. I hope to use my knowledge to steer you in the right direction.

But I want to make one thing very clear: *you* are the songwriter. *You* come up with the words that matter the most to your heart, and the rest will fall into place (provided you have all the tools necessary to flesh it out).

This will help you in visualizing how the creation will sound. The music and the lyrics merge like a marriage. Give yourself extra points if you happen to be a *singer* as well, because, at its core, you know how it's going to sound. All you need to do is sing it!

The next few chapters will prime that God-given creative brain of yours to be in sync with songwriting. Confidence is absolutely key. If you're not confident in your words, please believe this: it will show in your writing and performance.

Some tools, tips, and tricks include a helping of music knowledge to know how your words will fit into a framework, but don't lose out on *originality* – not by any stretch. The structure of a ballad has been time-tested, in other words. You can most likely fit *any* set of words into a ballad without a problem, but that won't make a great song at all. So focus on originality the most. That will drive that creativity and confidence to a level you never thought existed.

Before we move on in your journey of becoming the songwriter you want to be, however, I want you to understand the purpose you're going to have. The practice of writing songs will be a kind of therapy that will benefit *you* for years. It did for me. When we *write a new song*, we are renewing our minds. Songwriting is one of the best methods of self-expression with lyrical poetry manifested in sounds we love to rest and heal the soul.

Just the knowledge that a song I wrote connected with others on a deep level is healing all by itself. So keep this in mind: definitely write for your audience, but above all else, write for *yourself*.

You are, after all, your best fan.

So without further ado...

PART I

1

ASK YOURSELF THE QUESTION: WHY SONGWRITING?

"What we want to do is not nearly as important as what we want to be."

—Charles R. Swindoll

It's good that you *want* to be a songwriter, but are you one? Only you can answer that. Typically doubt gets into the brain and you ask yourself all the *what-ifs* you can muster:

- *I don't sing well*
- *I'm not very creative*
- *What if people think my songs suck?*
- *I don't know how to play guitar*
- *Who's ever heard of a piano? Not me!*
- *I can't even dance. Who would want to dance to* my song??

Just *stop*. Stop criticizing yourself. Once you stop, you're already halfway there. So first off, ask yourself why you want to write a song? Is it just because you think it would be interesting? Or do you have an urge to express yourself? Or to impress someone (like your crush)?

Sometimes hearing music on Spotify, or on the radio, pushes you in the direction of having the desire to just *create* something. If that's the case, go with it. But here's what you need to remember: go with it <u>without thinking about what the end result will be.</u>

I call that the *being vs. doing* mindset. For each, there's a place in time.

Being a *Doer*.

Are you a doer? If so, you're more goal-oriented. You simply want to finish writing that song. And that's okay except for the fact that you're not preoccupied with discrepancies, focusing more on the actual versus the desire.

Being a... *Be-er?*

Doesn't sound as 'cool' as a *doer*, I know, but let's just call it the 'being' mode. Let's say you're in that mode. What are you more interested in? Creativity, openness, acceptance, willingness, simply wanting, not *pushing*.

Another way of thinking about a person in 'being' mode is that you don't struggle much with writer's block. You just let it flow with your soul, you know? You just go... Go into that place where you embrace the entire process without worrying over what you're going to get.

Who cares if the song sucks! You just want to *create*. That's where the sweet spot is. You get into that groove where you can hear it in your heart, those beats and that rhythm, and all of a sudden it all comes out without even thinking about whether the words are right, placed right, or sounding right to whatever the beat may sound like (because, remember, songwriting is just the development of those lyrics *without* the music to accompany them).

That's the difference you need to figure out:

Are you saying you *want* to be a songwriter? Or *are* you a songwriter?

Take note: if you're the latter, you give yourself the space you need to embrace the process. This keeps you from second-guessing yourself. In the end, you produce faster, more efficiently, and – best of all – more creatively.

Once you have that figured out in your head...

Consider the process... versus the results.

What do I mean by 'process'? The first question you need to ask yourself is:

Who am I writing this song for?

Are you writing it for your friend? Your mother? Your brother? Your teacher? *Yourself*? This may lead you to determine what's more important to you: the *results* or the *process* leading to those results.

If you're writing a song just for yourself, you then have to ask yourself *why*. For self-fulfillment? Expression? Just the sheer accomplishment of it? Please don't say 'accomplishment'. While, yes, it's an accomplishment, songwriting reaches far above and beyond that.

Songwriting is an opportunity for you to grow, discover parts of yourself you never knew existed, and maybe even explore the unknown!

Knowing that, ask yourself again... *Who am I writing this song for?*

Say *no one*. Not even for yourself.

This allows you to *trust* in the process alone, keeping in mind these three benefits that will help you create something that may speak to the world in a way only the *genius* Stevie Wonder could!

- You won't feel the need to 'rush'
- You'll definitely *enjoy* the process of songwriting
- And best of all, you'll *always* see the value in your work

It won't matter what others think or say. All that matters is the song does *exactly* what it's supposed to do – it'll whisk a listener away into another world of radiance, complete with manifested sounds of chords, beats, and rhythms that'll make anyone dance.

In fact, that's why you tell yourself the song is for no one – that means it'll be for *everyone* to dance to!

The next step: consider your intentions.

You've considered the 'being' mode and 'doing' mode. You've also looked at the *process* and *results*. Now ask yourself: *what are you doing it for?* Is it for growth? Or results? Look back on the fact that songwriting shouldn't simply be for the audience, but *you*.

If you're looking at being a songwriter to impress others, stop. If you're looking to be a songwriter so you can be a star... *stop*. Sure, that's an enticing extra 'benefit' in that your song can skyrocket on the charts, but know this: that's just an extra 'benefit'. Your real purpose? That's you. And you have to decide if you're willing to take the time you need to nurture that desire in you.

The creative process *all by itself* is the reward.

Don't get me wrong – we *want* a completed song. We simply need to work on creating it. Focus on that. In doing so, you pour that part of your heart and soul into the *creation* of the song, first and foremost. By doing that, you let go and get whatever burdens you're holding off your chest.

In fact, have you ever noticed how many songs out there seem to reach into deep, intense, dark, hurtful, and healing places? That's no coincidence. Most songs are written by those who need to heal somehow. And I can guarantee this: *everyone* needs to heal over *something*. Why not benefit from the process and then marvel at the absolute creation?

Okay, so can I dream *big* or not?

It depends on what you mean by 'big'. Here's an example:

Let's say you visited the pyramids of Egypt and marveled at their magnificence. You were so enthralled by them that you just had this *urge* to recreate them in a painting, and you weren't going to sleep until you managed to manifest all of them in their majesty on canvas.

We can call that a 'big' undertaking. That's going *big*. Name anyone who even considered managing such a massive project. The interesting thing to note is that you're not necessarily doing it for anyone but yourself. That's the key characteristic to always remember.

You're going 'big' – but for yourself. There's nothing wrong with that. By all means, go *big*!

But don't go 'big' just to be *bigger* than others. It's not a competition. If it's going to be a competition, make *yourself* the opponent. Go bigger *every* time you approach songwriting – excel beyond what you've done previously. Songwriting is a craft just like any other art form. You train in it. You elevate your art with it.

That's why we're called music *artists*.

Are you a music *artist*? If so, you're going to need the next chapter, for sure. Because it will address one of the bigger questions you might have about whether expertise in the music industry is a must.

2

WHY YOU DON'T HAVE TO BE A 'MUSIC GENIUS' TO WRITE A GREAT SONG

"I haven't understood a bar of music in my life, but I have felt it."

—Igor Stravinsky

And what a remarkable quote that is when you realize who Igor Stravinsky is: one of the most influential and innovative composers, pianists, and conductors of the 20th century. Striking how we see that he himself admits that he *never* "understood a bar of music" in his life. But here's the key to what he's saying:

He felt it. And that's really all you need.

Many musicians have felt the same way. It's a stirring inside that makes you want to express yourself. Artists like Eminem made it very simple: "Sporadic thoughts will pop into my head and I'll have to go write something down, and the next thing you know I've written a whole song in an hour."

The act of it is so basic. Real. Raw. Anyone – literally *anyone*

– can do it. You most certainly don't need to be a scholar with music to be a songwriter, but understand this:

Some knowledge does help.

What you're going to explore in this chapter is how to be inspired, what to do when it hits, and how to start writing even when it *doesn't* hit.

Let's first start with the major facts here: you've listened to music. Quite possibly your entire life. The fact that your body has been an utter witness to the power of music – and the power of words behind it – is the catalyst for how you're able to express it. It's a give-and-take. A two-way channel of the free flow of ideas as songs touch you in truly intense ways. Think about it:

- What are your favorite songs? I'm sure you have a lot!
- *Why* are those songs your absolute favorite? You do have a unique reason. Trust me.
- Now imagine *relating* to those songs on your own personal level.

Congratulations: there's a songwriter inside you. Because *every* songwriter before you has been inspired by the work of others. Hands down, that's the truth.

Beyoncé was inspired by Diana Ross and Anita Baker. Guaranteed. Michael Jackson and Prince were both inspired by, you guessed it... *James Brown.*

Every songwriter *and* singer in all of existence has experienced that inspiration, that drive to make something their own *without* the need for, well, for lack of a better term, *musical genius. There* then exists the musical genius from within without the need for theory, knowledge, practice, training, or even a college degree.

So don't deceive yourself: you're no less than the greats in our music history, for sure.

Nevertheless, this book will guide you through the basics of what it takes to play on a keyboard or even a guitar.

All it takes are a few chords to understand the sounds that come out of what you play. Composing a song comes from the inside – what you *hear*. An instrument? That simply *helps* you hear what's inside perhaps a little 'better'!

So take advantage of it. Leverage the technology out there. It's remarkable what kind of apps you can find on your phone that allow you to make beats and sounds, incorporating an *entire* composition from start to finish.

And wouldn't you know it: you did it all without being a 'genius'.

That being said, pay close attention to when inspiration strikes.

Expect the unexpected as an artist. You've probably heard that everywhere. Our brains are strange like that. As you live your life, you will become inspired, but it will be during the strangest times – perhaps in your sleep – or even in the strangest places (like the bathroom).

That's normal. Take it in stride.

Before you start thinking that it would be tremendously cliché and stupid that your ideas would hit you at the oddest times and locations, take note:

Paul McCartney came up with some of his best songs while he was dreaming. Mariah Carey came up with the chorus of her smash hit "Hero" on her way back from the bathroom.

So, once again... you're not alone. Not by a longshot.

Given that inspiration tends to hit like a ton of bricks when you're not paying any attention, you need certain tools to keep you prepared. These tools aren't terribly expensive, nor are they exclusive to musicians and composers.

In fact, chances are pretty good you already have these tools on your phone!

Here's what you're going to need:

- A notebook (or an app that allows you to take notes)
- A recorder (which, as you may have guessed, exists right on your phone)

That's it. Pretty easy.

Here's the thing. While I've spent some time discussing this with you, the idea that inspiration can be this driving force of ingenious revelation... *it's overrated*.

Here's why 'inspiration' doesn't cut it in today's songwriting world.

You'll most likely be waiting for years to be inspired. This doesn't mean you're *not* a songwriter. In fact, it may mean the complete opposite. What many artists do (in fact, probably *all* artists do this without even realizing) is *invite inspiration in*.

It means putting yourself in *front* of inspiration – like you're on the railroad tracks, and inspiration is that bullet train about to hit you. Don't be afraid of it. Just run right into it. Trust me. The power behind it will shock you.

Why is that? *Inspiration comes from discipline.* Case in point: authors, novelists, dancers, painters, etc.

The *only* way you can train, practice, and grow as an artist is to simply *do it*. Don't stare at the canvas, waiting for something to happen. Just do *something*! Even if it's crap. The simple act of making your body move – or sing, or write, or play, or *anything* – is the pure invitation for inspiration to hit.

Pick up that guitar. Start strumming some notes. Get that pencil and paper. Write some thoughts down. Discipline yourself to know the difference between instant gratification and the true art form of songwriting.

I make no bones with you on it: songwriting requires patience. Hard work. Blood, sweat, and tears. It won't simply *happen*. Sometimes you have to work hard to make it happen. And before you know it, you strike gold with something so profound, infectious to the ears, and absolutely *dying* to be made into a song.

That's hard work worth every second of your life.

That being said, your *mood* certainly will play a role.

But not in the way you think. What do I mean by that? Think of all the kinds of songs you've heard on the radio. How many are about love, nature, pain, fear, sadness, happiness, or well... *anything*?

That's no accident. Your *mood* plays a role, but not as a challenge. It's a guide. Let your mood dictate how you accomplish the best work – not the other way around. If you let your mood *impede* you, you're going to be running in place, not getting anywhere. That's death to a songwriter. Avoid it like the plague.

Be prepared that the technicalities of what makes a great song will be explored in the second and third parts of this book; but for starters, what you'll need to know first and foremost is that the song you create will be born from the mood you're in, the period of life you're experiencing, and how you project that on paper.

The most important thing to remember about that is, whatever mood you're in, *authenticism* will be key in reflecting the highest quality in your songs.

- If you're sad about your best friend being sick, the song you're going to write will be about that.
- If you're excited about your first kiss, your song will be about the feelings behind it.
- If you're annoyed about your roommate being noisy while you sleep, your song will be...

That's right: it will be about *that*. Not always literally, but emotionally, mentally, and maybe even spiritually. That's what authenticism is all about.

How does that translate to musical composition, though?

Given that you've listened to music, you might also notice a link of how sounds will *sound* to you. This gives you direction on what perhaps *fear* will sound if you were to hear it in a song.

Take Eminem, for instance, and the duality he often portrays. Some of his rap songs are, in fact, rather punchy, quippy, and downright hilarious. Others, though, bring out the darkness in him. That's not an accident. When he writes, it often finds its way on paper completely based on the mood he's in the moment he's writing it down.

You'll often hear dissonance in some chords, or minor chords, which will dominate as you think about pitch and tone when thinking of sad songs or angry songs or confusing songs or just downright *scary* songs. That's okay. It's perfectly fine *because* that's authentic with the mood.

Dissonance is, in fact, an aspect of musical theory. It evokes an emotion.

Major chords, however, achieve the opposite. They sound

positive. Did you ever wonder, in fact, why they're called 'major' and why minor is called 'minor'? The connotations are striking. We get a sense of something that is *major* as profoundly influential in a way, and minor is, well... *not*.

Hence why major chords tend to result in happier and more optimistic songs. They don't jam the senses in a way that's jarring, or disparate. They synchronize well. They match well. They are completely *well* with your soul, and that's the whole point. Likewise, the words accompanying the song will then also go well with whatever's being sung.

- Think of "Isn't She Lovely" by Stevie Wonder
- Or "Faith" by George Michael
- Or "No More Drama" by Mary J. Blige
- Or "Happy" by Pharrell Williams

Many more examples out there in the music industry exist, which is why we get to the next part here: *listening*. Above all else, listen to what's around you. Sometimes you might bump into inspiration all on your own – just by listening.

3

STOP. LOOK. AND LISTEN.

"People ask me how I make music... it's like stepping into a river and joining the flow."

—Michael Jackson

Don't look at this chapter merely on the surface. I'm not saying just listen to every song you hear on the radio and try to emulate it all. You miss the point of inspiration and especially originality, trying to – for lack of a better term – *copy* what you hear.

However, there *is* some value to managing a cover of something that has been so incredibly popular, but only to a point. Once you get to that point, you have to go *further*.

You get further by listening with *all* of your senses. Touch, taste, hearing, seeing, smelling. Access all of it, and you accelerate inspiration in a way that's remarkable. You might pinpoint an idea that's never been explored, and from there, your writing expands to a real story people may identify with. That's like a golden nugget.

Start with listening to your favorite songs.

The key in leveraging what's currently out there is knowing how to make something your own. Here are some incredible examples many never realized. Take the Beatles, for example. Did you know Chuck Berry was an inspiration for the Beatles?

What about Aretha Franklin? Her inspirations were none other than Sarah Vaughan and Mahalia Jackson!

We wouldn't have had the Beatles invading America with their infectious music had it not been for what inspired them along with the soul of Aretha Franklin all around the world. But what separated them from the inspiration was their own *invention*, their own unique *personalities*.

It kills me that many don't even know that Prince hardly could even read music! But he didn't have to. He simply had *ears*. What he heard touched him deeply enough to unlock the songwriter in him.

Truly this is what I mean by covers you could perhaps develop your own lyrics to. This spurs creation, intensifies inspiration, amplifies invention, accelerates ingenuity in injecting your own heart into what's been created before.

The point is to get a jump-off point that'll get you running from there. The rest may be all downhill. Who knows? You may come up with something so original that it may define an entirely new future generation of musicians! If that doesn't make you a songwriter, I don't know what will.

Always remember that it's not just about listening to music.

You find the most originality in your music by living and breathing, observing all the things around you. Not just on the surface, but deep down.

Take for instance a homeless lady feeding the birds in Central Park of New York City. Observe her and what she does.

- Why does she do it?
- What's going on in her mind?
- Why is she homeless?
- Does she care if she's homeless?
- Why does she care or not care that she's homeless?
- What do the birds represent for her?

Before you know it, you have the components of what can be a great song. It's a *story*. It may or may not have a singular beginning and end, or even a conflict at heart, but it's a story about a *person* who's *real*. When it comes to songwriting, that's all you need: you need *real*.

Now constructing the song around the words you've built? That's a separate task, but an easy one if you already have an emotion inside you ready to be woven into the sounds you hear or feel.

Sounds great, but what if there's not much to listen to?

Here's the secret: explore.

Go for a walk. Find places that stir some emotion in you to the point where you feel the need to write something down. Or even hum something that's particularly unique.

When that happens, you just might have found a *hot spot*. It's a space where you get into your 'zone' – that place where creation is born. Your senses will be at their most optimal. You can then tap into the deepest parts of your creative mind and come up with the words that can make a great song.

Other general tips include:

- Plan your writing time out accordingly
- Record your thoughts as you think them
- Don't censor or judge yourself at all
- Set daily goals (and be absolutely militaristic about it)
- Clear the 'clutter' every day (you'll need time to basically do *nothing!*)
- Daydream (you heard right: just stare out the window and dream of unicorns or something)
- Let your recorded or written-down thoughts simmer

Once you have a routine down, you'll discover something remarkable – that common myth called writer's block? It will cease to exist. You'll come up with ideas that could expand and evolve into a song that'll indeed be catchy in its own right.

Rinse, repeat, rinse, repeat, rinse, repeat. Just remember: the artistic process is a trial-and-error concept brimming with effort. Take note of this one important point: most of your songwriting will always be working *inside your brain.*

The actual writing? That happens *after* you've discovered the overall theme, structure, main idea, concept, focus, or story.

Understand that you'll most likely fail a hundred times with false starts, clunky words, and rather dry concepts. That's okay. Don't sweat it. You'll most likely conjure a thousand more duds than treasures, and it will be a numbers game. It's a process of evolution. The more you do it, the higher the treasure-to-dud frequency ratio. Songwriting is a craft. Exercise it like a muscle.

Sounds painful... Am I just going to be a 'tortured artist' constantly listening to everything that hurts or heals?

Absolutely not. In fact, you *definitely* don't want to be. Why? Because it's a myth.

Here comes the idealized glamour behind the theory of the *tortured artist*, a popular myth that says you *have* to have issues in order to create. Not true. It's easy to get into that headspace, though, as you discover that oftentimes you have to struggle with something to write about it.

But a struggle isn't the same thing as a problem you have: like alcoholism, drug addiction, affliction, or instability in your life.

Don't go out of your way to make yourself poor, so you can see and feel what it's like to be in that space. Don't willingly involve yourself in unhealthy relationships, so you can explore what happens to your mind and therefore know how to write about it.

You'll always struggle with something. So focus on *those* struggles, *not* on what is particularly dark, awful, difficult, painful, or just downright agonizing. Instead of being a tortured artist, be a *stronger artist*.

You'll have intense feelings about anything that'll cause some conflict within yourself, but you'll have the strength to work through them in very healthy ways. And you'll most definitely know exactly how to express those feelings. In fact, that may be part of the therapy you may need to work through them.

Common affirmations you might tell yourself:

- *If my life gets better, my work's going to be boring and I'll have no 'edge'.*
- *If I get too content with myself in my life, I just won't be motivated.*
- *Well, what about Kurt Cobain or Amy Winehouse? They struggled!*

Chances are good we've all said at least one variation of any of these if we have this innate desire to create, to be songwriters, poets, artists, dancers, painters, etc. We *want* to have that stamp of character on our forehead that says we've struggled, carrying regret our entire lives.

So, okay, sure, you might turn over interesting work when you're depressed. Maybe even drunk. But does that mean you *don't* turn over interesting work when you're doing just fine? Do you *have* to have problems to be creative? Absolutely not.

Moreover, when we hear the songs at the campfire written by the 'tortured artist', what do we immediately think? "Wow, you must've gone through so much hell to come up with something so powerful."

Possibly... but what if that tortured artist really didn't? Then what? What if, in fact, that tortured artist was perfectly fine *in the midst* of struggle – and better yet – was perfectly fine *afterward*, proving that the song is a celebration and not a reminder of how crappy life can be?

That is conceivable. That is realistic, too. We can't assume the negative. Anything's possible. And quite honestly, as a songwriter, I'd rather opt for positivity. You know what they say... "You can't see the stars without the darkness around them."

As for being 'too happy', I'd wager to say that it's not even possible to attain that level of perfection. So why worry about it? Chances are good you won't be *too* happy.

There will always be some form of struggle for you to explore and imagine, to create something that *may be*, *could be*, *might be*. Perhaps you'll imagine the *worst* and also write about how you have the strength to combat it. It might even motivate you more when you realize that there will *always* be that possibility: your life may take a turn for the worst, you will face a challenge or two, or adversity will strike.

Here's the thing about tortured artists such as Kurt Cobain or Amy Winehouse. Geniuses, they were, but imagine what life would be like if they *hadn't* killed themselves. Ask yourself the important question: *would they still be creating masterpieces?* Probably. Let that sink in.

You don't need to hit rock bottom to create masterpieces. You might want to be able to know what rock bottom looks like, but you certainly don't have to have a one-way ticket to rock bottom just to ensure inspiration in writing songs of woe or wiles.

Okay, sounds great... now what?

Start listening. The question is how to start. We now know *where*, but now we need to know *how*. Here are some preliminary strategies to try (and fail, most likely, but hopefully succeed!):

- Step 1: Find a message you're absolutely passionate about.
- Step 2: Choose a simple melody (and it literally could be anything that comes to mind).
- Step 3: Think of how that melody can *change* and *expand* (add new notes, pitches, tones).
- Step 4: Find a place to write where you can be *completely* alone (no distractions).
- Step 5: Pick up an instrument (it doesn't have to be a piano. It could be your voice or even rocks to bang around).

And last but not least... just have some courage within yourself to start creating!

4

AS YOU CREATE, YOU MAY COME ACROSS SOME SETBACKS. DON'T SWEAT THE SETBACKS.

"I will not lose, for even in defeat, there's a valuable lesson learned, so it evens up for me."

—Jay-Z

Remember when I mentioned failure? That'll happen often. That's separate from a *setback*. A setback is *not* a failure by any stretch. You may face a setback and succeed in overcoming it, but you'll fail if you *don't* overcome it. Failure's always an option, and you'll always learn from it. A setback, though, may set you up for the worst.

They're typically called obstacles. They impede you from accomplishing what you want to accomplish. As a result, you might not even bother trying for fear of failure. That's what this chapter is all about: avoiding the setbacks you'll face in your life.

Setback #1: I don't have the time to do this.

Of course, you don't. It's a priority thing. We all have responsibilities. By chance if you have some free time on your hands, and you're *not* spending that time writing a song, chances are pretty good you actually don't really *want* to write that song. That's just a matter of fact.

Or it could be an excuse.

In my case, if it was the latter, I'd be pretty angry with myself!

However, sometimes it's just extremely exhausting to devote yourself to the art of songwriting. Your brain might need a recharge after the day of errands, the 9 to 5 job, dealing with customers and clients, going to the grocery store, and arguing with other people constantly. By the end of the day, you just don't have the strength.

If that's the case, I can understand that it's simply not an excuse. It's a challenge. Think of this as another challenge for you to overcome. Like with anything that involves an art form... even when you don't feel like doing it, just *do it*.

You'll grit your teeth, you might end up feeling not so confident, but what you might notice is that *after* a session of songwriting, something's going to happen to you: it's called *motivation, energy, passion, drive*. Once you're done, your brain won't stop. It'll actually keep *going* until the next time you sit down and start writing.

It's like a domino effect. Once you knock down the first one, if the second one's close by and gets knocked over, that's two. Once it knocks the third, that's three, once it's next to an entire line of dominos, hey, you've got a cascade!

Don't be surprised if it gets easier and easier as you keep working at it – even when you're already exhausted.

Setback #2: I don't know how/I won't make anything good!

By now, you're seeing a trend: these setbacks aren't really *environmental*. They're more psychological. These setbacks you often place in front of yourselves on purpose for whatever reason:

- Doubt
- Fear
- Anger
- Annoyance
- Lethargy
- Pain

Truly a whole host of issues might crop up, keeping you from doing what you really want. And some of these issues might be quite debilitating. But saying you just "don't know how"? Look yourself in the mirror and ask this question: *Does that mean I can't try?*

Of course not! Who says you can't try? Not me. Not you. No one. If *you* are telling yourself that, then that's a completely different issue you'd need to address. That has nothing to do with not knowing how. That's whether you think you're able to *learn*.

More importantly, just embrace the unknown! Expand your knowledge. Watch something unfold, evolve, grow. The reward of doing that would be magical. Astronomical. Even spiritual. Honestly, I feel closer to God when I'm making music.

Plus what's the definition of a good song anyway? Imagine you're Jackson Pollock, for instance – the artist who thought splashing cans of paint on a canvas would be considered art – and ask yourself what makes a great work of art and would it matter to you if someone *else* looked at your work and said, well...

"Hey, that's just a canvas with paint splattered all over it. That's not art."

Well, to *you*, that's not art. To *me*? That's treasure.

In that same vein, ingenuity with art is completely subjective, so the reality is no one can say that *this* song written by Bruno Mars, or *that* song written by The Notorious B.I.G., is any good or not. Don't make it about 'bad' or 'good'. Make it about *you* and what it means to *you*.

Understand that you may turn over a 'bad' song here and there, but it won't break you. It won't be a permanent stain on your history. Guaranteed, the most prolific and popular of artists have turned in some duds, but for every ten duds or so that ended up being fillers in albums, there was at least a hit single or two that swept a nation and changed lives.

Songwriting relies on the law of averages. Think of it like a deck of cards. Keep turning cards over (also known as songs) until you hit the ace.

Setback #3: But I don't know what to write about!

Ask yourself a different question instead of *what should I write about?* That almost invites the mythical creature, writer's block, to your door.

What happens is as your brain thinks of what you *should* write about, you're then thinking of all the possibilities, wondering what you should choose. Literally dozens of possibilities creep up in your brain... *Where do I start?* you think, right? The ordeal is overwhelming.

The question you *should* ask isn't "What *should* I write?" – it's "What *can't* I write?"

First, consider what you care about in your life. Your pet, your family, your friends, your faith, your dreams, your money, your addictions, a relationship, a social issue, working out, running, dancing, eating tacos, watching the NBA, playing GTA.

You might not realize it, but you've listed literally dozens of potential candidates for a song, and they're *all* worthy. Just keep telling yourself that: *I don't need to pick. I only need to <u>do</u> it!*

Just try this exercise:

1. Get a paper and pen.
2. Write about *whatever* for at least five minutes.
3. Don't stop writing during those five minutes.
4. Even if what you're writing about makes absolutely no sense!
5. Then choose your *favorite words* and *sentences* out of what you've written.

Your favorite words or sentences could be...

- Apples
- Bubble baths
- Did I remember to text my friend back?
- Turkey sandwich sounds really good.
- Picasso

Congratulations. You now have something to write about. The scary thing is I'm willing to bet you could incorporate all of this into one song...

(If you can, you've most likely accomplished what this book has tried to help you with, and you may put it down now and start creating!)

Setback #4: I'm not talented enough.

Who told you that?

If it wasn't you who said that, know that anyone else *cannot* judge that based on simply measuring you. It's, in fact, not possible for anyone – even the great Smokey Robinson – to say that you're just not a good songwriter. Someone might say that it's an *opinion*, but not the whole objective *truth*.

My mentor, the award-winning singer, and songwriter, Kim Burrell, once told me, "Mateo, you will never please everyone in the room. And that's okay."

In other words, don't compare yourself to others. Work harder than the most talented, and nine times out of ten, psychologically you'll always come out on top. The trick or challenge is to ensure that *you* are the one who always works the hardest. Just imagine your back's always against a wall, and you have no choice but to move forward. No moving backward.

When your work ethic is *that* die-hard, chances are pretty good you'll always be one step ahead of the competitive game regardless. Keep practicing.

It's all worth it in the end.

But guess what... this isn't the end. You're about to enter the gauntlet, but it's going to be so beautiful. It's time to start writing.

PART II

5

A QUICK LESSON ON SONGWRITING STRUCTURE

"I start with the music..."

—John Legend

The irony is that's what we normally think of when we actually start to construct a song from start to finish. Within the context of what John Legend once said about his process, many begin with the music while some find it easier to start with the idea of the song or even write the lyrics first.

The point is to just *write*. Let the creative mind guide you in *how* you write the song. The *structure* of that song then will be an integral part of the composition almost naturally, organically.

Here's the thing about songwriting: knowing the structure of a song certainly does help the process *move*. You begin to understand it more. And sometimes the structure a song *should* take will in fact be a source of inspiration when you're hitting a roadblock.

So does the sound come first? Or do the lyrics come first?

Neither. You might come up with a melody that strikes you, and *that* may inspire the lyrics to go with it. Or you might think of a title or a very poetic phrase of some kind that will then expand to the verses and bridge and so on and so forth, then a melody will somehow attach itself to it as you sing it to yourself.

There's no telling what will happen as a song begins to be born. That's part of the joy of it all.

You'll even get to ask the question of whether you're able to develop the melody *and* the lyrics independently of each other, fitting them together at the very end. It's possible. It would be challenging... but possible. The important thing is that your song, however it's created, will originate from a very deep, personal space, and as long as you're true to it, the finished product will be just as true.

I like poetry... but can a poem be a song?

I love this question so much, because it stems from an evolution of what it means to *write* – versus *perform*.

All poetry can be, to some degree, enjoyed in written form. But songs? They *have* to be performed. You write a song with the *purpose* to be performed. That then means if a poem *must* be performed, especially with music, it should have a format that's conducive to that kind of performance.

- It must have rhythm
- They must be written in very distinct lines
- It must be organized into actual sections (which we'll get to shortly)
- Generally speaking, if it's short and condensed, it can easily be a three-minute song

- And it has to be rich in rhythmic technique (rhyme, repetition, etc.)

Understanding the basic sections of a song.

1. First, there's the *intro*

Every song has a version or variation of this particular section. It's the beginning. Most of the time it's a slow build with words or sounds of the singer establishing the rhythm, tempo, and melody. It's the setup. Typically, it'll be at a slower pace and more low-key than the rest of the composition.

2. Followed by the *verse*

This section often resembles a poem. It will tell a story, sort of like the first chapter of a book. But it will tell it in such a way that it's melodious, harmonious, rhythmic. If you really analyze many songs, such as Frank Ocean's "Thinking About You" or TLC's "Waterfalls", you'll notice that a verse tells a specific story, introducing you to the main idea of the whole song.

3. The *pre-chorus* then might follow

Always optional but highly effective, this section aims to lead into the next one with a chord progression strictly from what follows it as a way to build upon the familiarity. Generally speaking, you can use a pre-chorus as a way to experiment, utilizing different harmonizing just to break up the pattern of the song and have the chorus stand out even more. So don't be afraid to use it.

4. Already mentioned... the *chorus*

The whole point of the chorus is to make it clear *why* the initial verse was sung in the first place. It drives the point home. This is the whole truth of the song. A listener most likely will go *AHA!* – so *that's* what this song is about. Consider the very first time you hear TLC's chorus of "Waterfalls", and it'll make a whole lot of sense to you. A cautionary tale that you "don't go chasing waterfalls... Please stick to the rivers and the lakes that you're used to... I know that you're gonna have it your way or nothing at all, but I think you're moving too fast."

5. Perhaps the *post-chorus*

A less common short section. It maintains or cranks up the sonic energy from the chorus and serves as a link back to the verse. In most cases, the post-chorus contains few lyrics, repeating either the song title or another phrase, and extends the chorus by providing an additional memorable hook. Rihanna's "Diamonds" is a clear example of it. Occasionally, this section could also double as a lyrical and melodic intro or outro.

6. And then the *bridge*

Of course, before you get to this bridge, you're often continuing with the story you started in that first verse, followed by a repeat of the chorus. You can see there's an inherent rigid structure to a song that's not unlike, say, a sonnet in poetry. And before this bridge, you might have more than two verses, continuing the story.

The purpose of the bridge, however, is to change the pace or set up the climax of the song. Not necessarily the pitch or tone or rhythm, but most of the time it is. Just to switch it up a bit.

Taking the same example of TLC's "Waterfalls", the bridge is commonly the section of the song where Left Eye goes into her rap session, leading up to the ultimate finale of the song.

7. The *outro*

That's similar to the *intro* for obvious reasons. The intro goes *in*; the outro goes *out*. It's the conclusion. It's how the song will end. Most of the time, the outro is a simple repeat of the chorus with a few subtle changes to suggest that this song will end. Sometimes the outro is very specifically structured to signify a real *ending*. Other times, it's just a slowdown of what the intro was. What dictates how the song ends is how the song began, what the song is about, and how the song is paced.

Okay, so that's great: now what do I do with all of these sections?

Glad you asked. This is the fun part (believe it or not). The answer to your question is... *anything you want* (within reason, of course).

The fact is there are several variations of how to structure all the required sections of a song. Some of the most common are:

1. **AABA (32-bar form or Verse/Verse/Bridge/Verse)**

Dominant in the first half of the 20th century, this gets cutting edge, doing away with probably the most iconic structures in music today: it completely throws away the chorus. The structure does make up for that with each and every verse beginning or ending with a refrain, which is a one to three or so line repeated throughout the song. Oftentimes that refrain, in fact, is the title. The 1950s and 1960s employed this form, especially with rock music.

Examples of this structure include:

- "Over the Rainbow" by Harold Arlen and Yip Harburg
- "Black or White" by Michael Jackson
- "All I Want for Christmas Is You" by Mariah Carey
- "Don't Know Why" by Norah Jones

This form, however, remained dominant until the next came into prominence:

2. Verse-chorus form

As a more modern structure seen often, this form sees use in various genres, but it's particularly common in hip-hop and folk. The contrast is that the chorus (sometimes with a pre-chorus elevation) plays much more of a key role, differing in both rhythm and melody.

Famous examples of this form include:

- "Never Too Much" by Luther Vandross
- "California Love" by 2Pac
- "Love Lockdown" by Kanye West
- "No Problem" by Chance the Rapper

So many artists employed this form until future pioneers began to experiment with this variation below:

3. ABABCB (Verse/Chorus/Verse/Chorus/Bridge/Chorus)

Deviating from the standard verse-chorus structure, this

form utilizes the infamous bridge as a way to ramp up to the climax of the song. With that extra drive toward emotion, these artists got to benefit from it:

- "Rumour Has It" by Adele
- "Adorn" by Miguel
- "Hotline Bling" by Drake
- "When" by Kirk Franklin featuring Kim Burrell and Lalah Hathaway

And *still,* there are a couple of other variations. Another popular one was:

4. No bridge or chorus (AAA or Verse/Verse/Verse)

Full of ambition, this is a structure not often used due to its tricky nature. Two of the anchors in any song are completely removed. The *only* thing such a song can stand on aside from verses would be similar refrains as in the previous form. Also, here the title often becomes the refrain, but without a doubt, the refrain has to be as distinctive as possible to maintain interest and focus. The traditional Christian hymn "Amazing Grace" and Bob Dylan's "Tangled Up in Blue" employ it with varying melodies to ensure the verses don't get too repetitive.

The honest truth is you have a wealth of creativity and invention here.

Feel free to experiment on song structure, governing sound, and emotion.

Just look at Queen's "Bohemian Rhapsody". *That's* a song transcending any traditional form, coloring outside of the lines and coming up with a style that's all unique in its own right. So it is completely possible that you can come up with a song that's, like...

ABBAACCABABABACCCCBAB

Have fun with it. But take note of this important tip: whatever structure you're designing, it *has* to make sense within the context of the story you're telling.

Think of it as construction. You're an architect, designing a building, and you want to make sure everyone in the building has a way to get to the third floor and back down. Don't create staircases going to nowhere, don't have doors that don't open to other rooms, and *definitely* don't make hallways with dead ends.

Now before you flip out at how complex all of this is, regretting not getting that music degree...

Know that the best way to construct your first song is by listening to other songs.

And thereby we go back to the tried-and-true adage that you must *listen*. Listen to what's out there. Analyze. Emulate. And here's a really key secret for you:

Write out the lyrics of your favorite song *so you can see how it looks on paper.*

This presents to you the ultimate blueprint on what *your* voice should look like based on another framework. This may even help you determine the kind of melody you want for your song. The key here is experimentation. Play with the notes. Improvise a bit. Make it your own. And then match it all together just to see how it sounds. If it sounds like candy to you, you may have something going.

But analyzing any song that's out there, you'll notice right away what is the intro, the verses, the chorus, the bridge, and the outro quite clearly.

You might even notice that your favorite songs seem to have

something in common with respect to the overall structure and pattern. That means your ears like what it hears with those particular compositions. It then may also mean the songs you'll write and compose will also sound good to you.

At that point, ask yourself these important questions:

- What's unique about the verses?
- What's unique about the pre-chorus?
- What's unique about the chorus?
- What's unique about the bridge?
- Where do the actual titles appear in those songs you like so much?
- What's truly bizarre or original about the entire composition?

This will give you interesting clues as to what makes a song so *evocative* by being something *no one* has heard before. Case in point... Queen's "Bohemian Rhapsody".

Don't hate me, though, because what you're about to read will clue you in on the best possible advice for this chapter.

Ready? Take everything you just read in this particular chapter – and I mean *everything* – and this is what you do with all of it:

Forget it exists. Imagine it's gone. You don't have to pay any attention to it at all.

Seems counterproductive given you've devoted so much time reading through all of it, and now here I am saying that it doesn't matter. Well, sort of.

The fact is truly good songwriting *shouldn't* follow any kind of rigid structure at all. Consider writing all by itself. Think of the likes of poets, authors like C.S. Lewis or J.K. Rowling – ask yourself if these authors *truly* followed the rules of grammar, structure, syntax, and punctuation to a tee, and more often than not you'll notice that many of these great masters often did break a rule or two.

The same goes for songwriting: once you know the rules... you're free to bend them. Maybe even break them.

The best songwriting comes from deep inside your gut. In the end, you'll have the knowledge this book presents, and in the background, they'll always be a guiding light off in the distance. But your *understanding* of that knowledge? That comes from your creative side. Keep that in front of you at all times.

6

MORE ADVANCED TOOLS TO SPICE UP YOUR SONGWRITING STRUCTURE

"If at first you don't succeed, dust yourself off and try again."

—Aaliyah

Simply knowing the structure is half the battle. A big part of the training is accessing all the potential tools you'll have in an arsenal built for lyrical battle. This chapter will explore just that, with detailed definitions and descriptions of:

- Hooks
- Rhyme
- Other forms of poetic device

Now the first two are arguably the most basic and necessary to an extent. The third? I just combined a multitude of specific forms that you can *choose* to implement into your songwriting, but they're not necessarily *required*. To be fair, the first two aren't technically required either – but in my opinion, you'd be hard-pressed to instill lyrical quality without some sense of a hook or rhyme to maintain rhythm and flow.

The main point behind all of this is that you'll have a plethora of creative options to employ. Ample experimentation, discovery, liberation – that's the goal here.

So what is a hook?

Follow me closely. Instruction just may get truly complex...

A *hook* in a song is arguably the most dynamic part of the entire composition. It's the part of the song that catches the ear. Think of it as a tagline like:

- *Just do it.* – Nike
- *Melts in your mouth, not in your hands.* – M&Ms
- *The breakfast of champions.* – Wheaties

In a way, the hook represents *everything* the song is about, summarizing the *aha* moment, the main idea, the theme, the focus, the point. It answers the 'question'. Whatever that question is? – it just depends on the listener.

Although, sometimes the hook is the part of the song you just don't expect. Ever listen to a song and get to the point where you go... "Oh, wow, this is awesome!" Chances are good you had just been 'hooked' by a part of the song that *reeled* you in. You now want to listen to the *entire* song for whatever reason:

- To hear more of the lyrics
- To see where the bridge might go
- To hear how creative the vocals are
- Or to just hear how the *story* of the song ends

Oftentimes, that hook is the difference between a good or bad song. Sometimes it's even the difference between a good or *great* song. You might actually catch yourself noticing that a song just didn't reel you in at all – maybe it was missing a hook and therefore didn't garner that much interest, so you skip it on Spotify or Apple Music and move on to the next track.

Of course, what didn't work for you might work for somebody else. That makes it all the better for you as a songwriter as you simply focus on *yourself* and what grabs *you*. If you're honest about it, chances are you'll grab others with the song – and the hook – and experience fame.

Now the *type* of hook may be something you want to consider depending on the story you want to tell or the song you want to sing. Types include:

I. The "melodic hook"

Quite possibly the most common hook in music today, the *melodic hook* exists in almost every single genre you can think of. Chances are you've heard these hooks without even realizing they're hooks. That's the beauty of it: they don't lend *too* much attention to themselves, so you can be immediately drawn in for the rest of the composition.

It often lends itself to a kind of sweeping melody, somewhat low-key but distinct in nature. They're relatively easy to pinpoint if you pay close attention to what grabs you. A great example of a melodic hook is Post Malone's "Rockstar" as he employs the use of a very noticeable 2-note motif that is then repeated multiple times for effect, which invites one major tip about hooks –

Repeat the hook in your song.

This helps anchor that song with the listener to easily identify it in a very positive way, which leads us to another helpful tip: you want your hook to be very pleasing to the ear.

2. The "lyrical hook"

Imagine the same *melodic hook* but with a voice added to it. That's what this particular hook is. However, the words of the *lyrical hook* aren't just any such words of a song, but instead do what I had just described, which is to speak to the overall messaging.

You want that lyrical hook to be memorable. Catchy. Infectious. Simple. But sweet. Sometimes you might want to invent a new word or phrase that invites curiosity, but that's only *one* focus for this type of tool.

More often than not, the lyrical hook may separate itself from the rest of the song. It might have a different rhythm. It also may be at a different pitch or tone. Whatever the case, you will *know* that what you're hearing is unique and therefore worth the time of your ears.

Some examples of a lyrical hook include:

- *"Ah, ha, ha, ha, stayin' alive, stayin' alive... Ah, ha, ha, ha, stayin' aliiiive"* by the Bee Gees
- *"Bless"* up by DJ Khaled (or even just the motif he constantly uses... *"DJ KHAAAALED"*)
- *"YOLO"* by Drake

It's like a flag waving in the air that you're meant to see. Once you see it, you know what you're up for.

3. The "musical hook"

Like the *melodic hook*, the *musical hook* opts to go with a riff or motif that's distinctive, but not necessarily melodic in nature. Most of the time it actually emphasizes a *type* of sound, or instrument, that is truly original and indicative of what the band represents.

It could be a banjo. Or a kazoo. Or a harmonica. It's that exact musical *sound* that then defines the song – and even the singer. The *musical* hook may also be a part of the *melodic* hook as well, which brings about another clever tip in employing the use of these devices:

Leverage multiple types of hooks into one hook.

That spices up the hook to make it even *more* memorable than it would be with just one type. Think of what the Bee Gees would be if their hook didn't have their classic voice paired with it. The melodic hook doesn't have the same 'punch' without the lyrical hook to go with it.

In that same vein, a musical hook can make a unique hook stand out even more. It can even be the pathway toward a Grammy solely on the ingenuity of using some clever instrument that's *never* been used before and somehow sounds quite interesting.

4. The "rhythmic hook"

Sometimes it's the beat that gets you. When you bop your head, do the 'air drum', or simply tap your foot. It's the hook without a melody, or a tone, or even a purpose until you realize that it sets the entire song up. That's what the *rhythmic hook* does, and there are a ton of examples of it out there in the music industry.

- "We Will Rock You" by Queen
- "Set Adrift on Memory Bliss" by P.M. Dawn
- "O.P.P." by Naughty by Nature

These songs are memorable for several reasons, but most notably you'd recognize these songs by a simple beat. The beat you'd hear is *so* catchy that oftentimes *other* artists then borrow that beat to employ in their own compositions – we call it sampling. In fact, P.M. Dawn's single samples drums and multiple elements from previous songs like The Soul Searchers' "Ashley's Roachclip" and Spandau Ballet's "True".

Other examples might include a particular beat that you wouldn't hear anywhere else – like with Naughty by Nature's "O.P.P." and the viral syncopation layered throughout the song. Instantly, you'd know what song it was from by the very beginning even *without* lyrics or other instrumentation. This phenomenon exists for a lot of songs, actually – and it is the stamp of musical infection that signifies a true hook.

Other genres employ it, too – like with hard rock. Queen took a cue from a motif that was purely inventive, using the simplest beat, but one an audience could actually participate in. The song itself became *the* rock anthem for decades solely based on the *one* set of beats anyone could do with their own feet and hands. Once again... *proof* that you can make music out of *anything* and have it be completely stellar, unique, and truly masterful.

5. Last but not least, the "sound-effect hook"

Instantly a winner if done right, with the right amount of subtlety. This one's not easy, but also easy to employ when you find something that's actually quite catchy. The rap genre utilizes this to great effect, but you better believe other genres focus on a type of 'sound' that can be distinctive, lending to the personality or brand of the music.

Some examples include:

- "Thriller" by Michael Jackson
- "Transform Ya" by Chris Brown
- "Walkin' On the Moon" by The-Dream featuring Kanye West

Here's a bit of an exam for you: find the "sound-effect hook" for each one of these. See if you can nail it. Here are some hints – one's all about horror, and the other two seem to echo everything science fiction!

Here we have another point to make regarding that: What if you don't like science fiction? What if you're not too big on horror movies? What if scratching on a chalkboard just isn't your thing?

You won't ever find a "universal hook" everyone will like.

It simply doesn't exist. Some dig those melodic hooks, and that's fine. Others identify with rhythm so much more. The important thing you have to realize is that each person represents a unique personality with a background and past experiences that will influence whether they'll like the song or not. So just *know that* – and don't take it personally if someone doesn't seem to jive with your composition at all *solely* based on the hook.

You won't be able to please everyone. So don't try.

As you've already guessed, hooks *can* be borrowed, repurposed, sampled, and expanded on – more often than not it's the lyrical hook that often never gets repeated from artist to artist unless there's something distinctive about the lyrics that set it apart from other pieces. You can substitute different words in a lyrical hook and have it produce the same effect, for instance.

The most important thing you'll want to do with hooks – regardless of the *type* of hook you're going for – is to *bait* a listener with it, making them think you're playing a simple chord progression once or twice, something predictable... and then you 'yank' the line with something *completely* different, steering the song in a different direction, an unexpected direction.

It's the difference between a song that's just 'fun' to listen to every once in a while... and a song that's game-changing, groundbreaking, trendsetting.

That hook you use will stand out, so use them sparingly. Imagine an entire song you've composed riddled with hooks – listeners will simply be overwhelmed with the convoluted inundation. They need something to hook their ears on as a basis, or foundation, for what they're about to hear for the next three minutes. Make it count. But make it simple and sweet.

What about rhyme? Do I have to be a poet?

It would help, yes, but you don't necessarily have to be Maya Angelou, Walt Whitman, or Robert Frost to write a song, by any stretch.

It's actually not hard to rhyme words. In seconds, you can probably come up with a dozen words that rhyme with each other, so stringing them together won't be too difficult except for the fact that you'll have to make the lyrics matter to the overall theme in a cohesive, understandable, and logical way.

Many, though, don't realize just how easy it is to rhyme. You don't *have* to be clever as a poet will be. You don't *have* to have full knowledge of all the words in the dictionary. Most of the time, you don't even need to use a thesaurus.

You simply need to know of words that sound *similar*.

What rhymes with 'similar'? Were. Cur. Sir. Blur. Fur. Sure. Perpendicular.

Don't necessarily think about *how* the rhyme needs to make sense with the theme of the song. The rhyme will only be a mere *component* of the song as a way to progress a beat and have it make sense within the context of the composition.

By all means, though, if the story you tell in a song can benefit from rhyme having a purpose *beyond* that of the beat and the rhythm, then go for it. Again, another reason why practice indeed makes perfect.

Thankfully, there are several *types* of rhyme to be aware of:

1. "Perfect rhyme"

The truest purebred form of rhyme, mimicking the exact vowel sound, followed by subsequent consonant sounds. In many ways, it's also the most difficult to make work in a song when you're trying to stick to a particular theme or story. Believe it or not, sometimes it's a detriment to manage *perfect* rhyme in a composition, lending a stiltedness and rigidity to your piece, which you want to avoid.

Sure, you can rhyme "cat" with "hat" and "that" without a problem, but *should* you? Probably not, but it depends on the song you're writing and how it will be performed.

2. "Slant rhyme"

Trickier. More subtle. But spicy in a way, too! The slant rhyme tones down the perfect rhyme by not sounding exact. Just *similar*.

In fact, let's go back to that word: *similar*. Sound it out, so you get a good grasp on what's supposed to be *rhymed* – it's an "er" sound. That's why all those other words (were, cur, sir, fur, sure, etc.) mimicked that *exact* sound.

But what about the word... *pure*? Or *lure*? Is that... *exact*? If you listen closely, you might actually say *no*. It's, in fact, not.

Similar sounds like "er". *Pure* sounds like "your". See the difference?

Working with slant rhyme gives you more access to words that aren't necessarily exact, but are similar enough to work within a melody. They still ring true to the ears, not so much mimicking the vowel or consonant sounds, but the *overall* sounds of the words instead.

3. "Masculine rhyme"

Masculine rhyme emphasizes *stressed* or 'dominant' syllables in a word. They're often the easiest, but also the most trite, to come up with. In fact, just about every basic one syllable word – like cat, dog, flog, nog, rat, smack, lack, back, tack, tuck, buck, suck, muck, mess, less, *stress* – is capable of a masculine rhyme.

For words that have more than one syllable, simply articulate the word and see where the *stress* falls. Such as... *profess*. Pro-FESS. Di*gress*. Di-GRESS. Un*less*. Un-LESS. If the emphasis is on the very *last* syllable, you're completing a masculine rhyme.

4. "Feminine rhyme"

The opposite idea applies as well. And creativity gets interesting here. A feminine rhyme is where the stressed syllable is *not* the last in the rhymed word, such as the word we'll go back to again here: *similar*. Sim*ilar*. SIM-ilar.

You rhyme with a feminine rhyme based on that last unstressed syllable, and as you've read, the word "perpendicular" is a perfect example. Perpen*dic*ular. Perpen-DIC-ular.

The creativity starts when you can, in fact, rhyme certain *masculine* words with *feminine* words without a problem:

- Confess
- Lioness
- Loneliness
- Caress
- Fess
- Recess

See if you can spot the feminine words – and the masculine words. They can all rhyme together, but there are *three* masculine ones – and *three* feminine ones.

5. And then the "end rhyme"

In a way, this last form of rhyme can encompass all forms of rhyme to a degree. The *end rhyme* is the *last* word in any line of text – whether it's in poetry or a song. It's distinctive in the sense that you can even rhyme – perfectly, slant, feminine, or masculine – *internally* within a line of dialogue about smog that seems to hog the rims of limelight so bright tonight...

- *Bright* and *limelight*... are internal feminine and masculine rhymes
- *Dialogue, smog,* and *hog*... are all internal masculine rhymes
- *Seems* and *rims*... are all internal masculine *slant* rhymes
- *Tonight*... is the end rhyme, but *only* if it is to rhyme with the next end rhyme in the next line!

Exhausting, yes. But creative? For sure. In fact, when you

speak, you probably don't even realize just how much you rhyme all the time. In fact, these rhymes of mine align with each line so well almost *automatically* due to understanding how the sounds match together so pristinely, serenely, and easily.

Here's another little test: pick out *all* the rhyming words in the past couple of pages in this book. All the perfect rhymes, slant rhymes, masculine rhymes, feminine rhymes, and end rhymes. Train your eyes to spot them. What you'll find is that as you scan more and more, you'll then be able to construct lines of text that will instantly rhyme so sublime that you'll be a true poet without even knowing it, seeing it, feeling it, or even comprehending it. It will become natural. Your language will *flow*. Your words will become *rhythmic*.

And so your songs will also be.

Now other tools you can use include:

- Repetition
- Alliteration
- Imagery
- Personification
- Simile
- Metaphor
- Assonance
- Consonance

These devices work together to amplify what you've already used in your composition, which is rhyme and hook.

I. Repetition

One of the easiest things you can do when composing a song

is to just repeat certain keywords that are in fact central to the overall structure.

Hooks work well with this for obvious reasons, not to mention repetition is used to great effect when repeating verses and choruses throughout an entire composition. Feel the flow as you intend to repeat certain words and see how the repetition fits with the mood, the overall emotion, and the intention you're trying to convey.

But don't repeat words *just* for the sake of maintaining flow or theme. Think of melody, for instance...

In *any* song, one single note may be repeated at least a dozen times. That's no accident. The fact is you'll *want* to repeat certain words just to amplify the natural flow of the song without disturbing it.

Think of the Bee Gees, for instance, repeating... "*Ah, ha, ha, ha, stayin' alive, stayin' alive... Ah, ha, ha, ha, stayin' aliiiiiiiiiiiiiiiive...*"

It wouldn't be as catchy to sing along to something like this if the Bee Gees decided that it would be better to instead sing... "*Ah, huh, oy, yo, stayin' alive, remainin' alive... Oh, yuck, 'sup, doh, stayin' aliiiiiiiiiiiiive...*"

It's harder to memorize. It's harder for an audience to identify with. It's just plain... *clunky*. The fact is repetition may be the true building block of songwriting.

2. Alliteration

For those who don't know what this literary device is, you'll most likely spot it like lovers living lowkey and loosely on a lavish land with lakes and doors locked to protect them from lanky losers looking to leave with personal items without them knowing it...

(Which letter was repeated over and over again? ...that's what alliteration is.)

3. Imagery

More abstract concepts lend themselves to descriptions of certain images to suggest some sort of emotion or theme. Another way of explaining this particular tool is to *show*, not *tell* – potentially something that could be truly effective in a song.

For instance: saying the color 'red' might, in fact, suggest everything from fire, to passion, to anger, to even an emergency. When you don't state the obvious, you give yourself the freedom to run with a word and leverage *not* its literal meaning, but its intended use to employ anything like a rhyme, or a hook, or alliteration, or anything else that would promote rhythm or the beat.

Don't ever discount imagery. It's the foundation behind songs that speak beyond the literal. And more often than not, songs that go beyond what's literally said in the lyrics tend to resonate the best with listeners.

4. Personification

Do *you* remember what "personification" is? If not, don't be ashamed. These are devices commonly taught back in grade school, but we never considered these being tools to use in song-writing.

Imagine your phone aggravating you. Maybe it's lagging or something. Perhaps it buzzed you into seeing that you only have a 5% charge left. That means it'll be going to sleep soon, and there's nothing you can do about it until you're able to get a charger. It means that shortly your phone's going to die.

The paragraph you just read happens to be littered with instances of personification. Do you see them?

Spotting them is easy: all you need to do is think *logically*:

- Can a phone *truly* and *intentionally* "aggravate" you?
- Can a phone *really* go to "sleep"?
- Can a phone *actually* "die"?

Literally, no. An inanimate object cannot do any of these things. People are aggravating. People go to sleep. People die. People laugh. People cry. Our actions as humans often define us and normally don't get associated with inanimate objects, electronic objects, buildings, plants, and even animals.

That's personification. You're *personifying* specific objects to add an additional layer of imagery, breathing *life* into them. We often tend to understand only ourselves as human beings. Personification allows us to understand other things with the same knowledge, which we employ to understand ourselves.

These days it's truly remarkable how often we use personification without even knowing it. Have you ever heard a fridge "growl"? I have. What about a sports car "gritting its teeth" at the starting line right before the race begins? Paints a very concrete and colorful image, doesn't it? That's because you're associating an emotion with the image, making that image so much more relatable.

5. Simile and metaphor

It's different when I say that the fridge is like a feral cat growling at me. It's also different when that sports car's a savage beast on the track, gritting its teeth. Not only are you *personifying* – you're now *comparing* and *contrasting* two different images, managing to visualize it on yet another layer. Take a wild guess on which comparison (the fridge or the sports car) is a simile and which one is a metaphor.

Again, this is another situation where you learn of this in grade school but never thought you could employ the use of it in something like songwriting. Nothing against poetry, but when writing a song, there's the potential for it being performed by you – perhaps even another artist! And if that's the case, the creative use of any of these devices, such as a simile or metaphor, may make all the difference.

Learning the difference between a *simile* and *metaphor* is simple: similes use "like" or "as" in their comparisons. Metaphors do not.

These are similes:

- I'm *like* the night sky during a thunderstorm: savage and tumultuous.
- She is *like* a heavenly angel, hypnotizing me as I dance with her.
- *As* a flower is to the desert, so am I without my water bottle.
- I ran *as* a gazelle runs away from a cheetah.

These are metaphors:

- I *am* the night sky during a thunderstorm: savage and tumultuous.
- She *was* a heavenly angel, hypnotizing me as I danced with her.
- I *am* a flower in a desert without my water bottle.
- I *was* a gazelle running away from a cheetah.

A question many ask is this: *which should I use and when?*

Why does this distinction exist anyway? Theoretically the simile and metaphor accomplish the same thing: they *expand* on the image to layer in more understanding of the visual. The distinction, though, serves certain purposes, especially in song-writing.

Maybe you need that extra syllable with your tempo. If so, you go with a simile. Perhaps the flow tends to work better as a metaphor? Then you go with the shorter line. If you notice, metaphors tend to be structured shorter depending on how the language operates.

If you're describing an action, often metaphors work really well. You visualize the action; you don't need to do much more, so therefore you don't need to say *like* or *as*, because the reader can see that already. However, if you're describing an emotion or condition, you might be inclined to stick with similes.

The message might change a bit between both depending on the context. Are you *really* the night sky, personified? And if so, *why*? It begs the question. If you're simply saying you're *like* the night sky, then there's no question as to why, because it's under-stood you're *you*, and the night sky is simply the... *night sky*. You just have certain characteristics of the night sky.

Is she *really* a heavenly angel (truly sent by God straight from heaven, basically)? Or is she just *like* a heavenly angel (meaning this song or story is about a new beautiful girl you met and are in love with), and you're just making a comparison between heaven and Earth?

Most of the time similes and metaphors can be flexible based on preference, but with the intention of communicating the idea in the best way possible. Some concepts are best expressed via simile; others are best expressed via metaphor. *All* concepts can be expressed either way, but you have to discern which would be the best way to employ based on how it sounds, what's being communicated and why.

6. And, finally, assonance and consonance

With strong ties to slant rhymes and internal rhymes, *assonance* (repeating the same vowel sounds over and over again) and *consonance* (repeating the same consonant sounds over and over again) really dig into the flow and sound of certain vowels and consonants to the point that an *entire line* can be melodious.

This is the case where it's not necessarily about rhyme as much as it is about how a line sounds in its entirety. Sure, certain words will rhyme when it comes to assonance and consonance, but *internally* they're hardly noticeable. It's more about how the sounds of certain words end up fitting together harmoniously.

Writing about your *inner issues* with *lemons* st*emmin'* from pro*blems* with smacking lips due to tart and tang may sound like one melodious rhyme, but you don't right away notice it until you think about it: that's assonance and consonance. The sounds of "in", "ons", and "em" (all of them sound similar to *in*) work together, tying the prose tightly in melodious fashion.

As a more intricate literary device, this takes tons of practice to incorporate in a song, deliberately editing and focusing on words that will synchronize better as a whole, fitting a melody, or overall sound of a song. Think of your composition as one big, elaborate jigsaw puzzle, and the word choice you employ are the pieces you're trying to fit.

Last, but certainly not least, you must be careful.

Beware of cliches. Beware of the dreaded "forced rhyme". These pitfalls are easy to drop into, and most of the time you don't even realize you're in them. That's not where you want to be by any stretch, but here's the worst of it: *they're very difficult to spot.*

What I mean is that it's *really* easy to go 'too far' with rhyme to the point that it's cliche. Sometimes you even fall prey first to a cliche and then sink even deeper as your rhyme scheme gets tired, trite, and empty.

That being said... think of the words "cliche" and "prey". They rhyme, don't they. So does the word "they". When you take your composition down that way, you can safely say that you've not gone astray toward a path of *been-there-done-that*, which every listener and reader nods their head in agreement – *"Yep, we've heard stuff like this before. This is just a sample. Or a rip-off. Not worth our time."* – but only to a certain degree.

Make no mistake that there's nothing wrong with imitation – to an extent. The similarities can be subtle with an advantage to you as you may sound *somewhat* like Lauryn Hill, for example. There will be enough interest in *you* and what makes you *unique* with the help of what is recognizable.

The good news is you may have noticed the key to avoiding trite and forced rhyme with ease simply by reading what you're currently looking at. After letting words like *cliche, prey, way, say,* and *astray* roll off your tongue, it's clear that *if* you're going to rhyme, make sure you're rhyming simply because the language – not *you* – dictates it.

There's a reason why they're called forced rhymes. You're *making* it rhyme. Don't. Let the language do it for you.

Oftentimes, it will happen naturally. If that's the case, then bravo. Other times you may need to research word choice a bit to see if you can massage the flow some to invoke that musicality into the words, as rhyme is known for doing. In managing that, you often avoid many cliches that have been heard before, like:

- "Down on my knees"
- "Now or never"
- "Cold as ice"
- "Love is blind"

And just about *any* line that's manufactured to rhyme with any of these...

Long story short, if a certain line gets plugged into a composition, and you *immediately* recognize it from some other well-known song, consider reworking it, or reinventing it.

And, yes, you *can* reinvent cliches. You *can* turn a "forced rhyme" into an *internal rhyme* or something like that, refreshing it and making it your own. The clever employment will be like a new candy a kid discovered at the supermarket.

(Did you catch that simile I just used?)

This is a lot of work... all this poetry stuff.

It can be, no doubt. However, you have motivation and creativity on your side. Don't let the challenge limit you. The bounds of your experimentation are infinite as you create, and here's how you avoid the doubt:

Invoking the "throw-away" policy.

Who said any first composition you create has to be the first song anyone will sing? It doesn't. *You* are the one in charge of your words. No one else has the right to sing them (except you). If you *want* someone to see it – and maybe sing it – then great. If not, that's great, too. There's a point to writing a song that never gets *seen* – or *sung*.

They're called throw-away songs. And they *do* have value contrary to the connotation within the label.

As an exercise, you won't experience anything more valuable. A song that you develop for the sole purpose of experimenting with, testing, trying, training, and practicing your craft will be the precursor to all your later masterpieces sung by the best nightingales of the music industry (and if you're one of those nightingales, even better).

Once you're done experimenting – in any fashion, it's

completely up to you – you simply *throw it away*. That's it. Chances are good you end up never seeing those words again.

Or perhaps... you *will*. It's all up to you. You are the master of your own words.

You, however, experience the blossoming of invention, opening new doors to originality by stumbling across calamities in your songwriting that are, in fact, real gems leading to the treasures that mean the most to you.

Which is what the next chapter will be about.

7

SONGWRITING WORKOUT SESSIONS TO GET THE BLOOD FLOWING

"Songwriting is a muscle.
The more you do it, the better you get at it."

—Jason Derulo

Think of the tools in the previous chapter as your machines for weightlifting. You have the bicep curl machine. The chest press. The shoulder press. The butterfly machine. Those tools help you focus your muscles into workout mode.

Sadly, those tools just sit there if you don't actively participate in the reps and sets, pushing you to the limit.

Indeed, songwriting is an exercise all on its own. It'll work you. The right tools will help work you well and with minimal recovery. The good news, too, is I have the *best* machines out there with the most optimal weight to help target the right songwriting 'muscles'.

The point, though, of these exercises isn't to just get better at songwriting; it's, in fact, to get more *unique* with your songwriting!

Here's where you find those gems behind those new doors...

Exercise #1: "Hand Puppets"

Might seem silly at first, which is why this is the first exercise you should try out. It'll break you out of your comfort zone. Get you into a *new* zone of discovery, cascading into the rest of these exercises with ease. Songwriting, in fact, *is* about discovering a new *you*.

More importantly, you might notice that this one is quite visual and not what you'd expect in any songwriting how-to book. I'd have to say that, without a doubt, you're touching on a unique aspect that may unlock the secrets of songwriting from within you *because* you're trying something new – you're experimenting, you're exploring, you're revealing.

And here's what you're going to reveal: your *left* hand will be a 'character' *you* create in your own head. This is where you get to be a storyteller.

Your *right* hand will *also* be its own 'character'.

What your right hand and left hand will do is have a conversation. Like *hand puppets*.

Here's the catch: they're going to have a conversation *solely* in rhyme.

I don't want you to get intimidated at all by this, because while some may have it easy with rhyme, others don't. That's okay. You'll find it's easy working yourself into it with simple and single words. What you have to understand is that the 'conversation' between your right hand and your left hand doesn't necessarily *make sense*.

Start with simple, singular words.

Let's say your right hand has a name: we'll call it "Benjamin". Your left hand will be "Jordan". They're face to face, having a 'conversation'. Here's an example:

Benjamin: "Conversation?"
Jordan: "Stimulation!"
Benjamin: "Hmm, situation..."
Jordan: "Education?"
Benjamin (wagging a finger): "Participation!"
Jordan: "Ugh! Emancipation!"

Feel free to keep going with it as long as you want until you feel comfortable verbalizing full sentences, turning it into a real conversation.

What you'll notice about the example is if you look up these words, you *might* see a point to all of them. It *may* point to an actual conversation these two are having.

Benjamin may be asking to have a chat with Jordan. Jordan exclaims with excitement! But Benjamin basically says there's a 'catch' (a "situation"). Jordan then begs the question: is this going to be a 'lesson'? Then, of course, Benjamin says, "Only if you participate!" Sadly, Jordan is disgusted, wanting *out* (wanting to be "emancipated") of the conversation, because he's not interested in having to be tested, instructed, lectured, or anything.

You'll notice it's quite easy to have a 'conversation' in your mind – and *knowing* how it can be expressed, even with just singular words. This primes you into really pushing your creativity in building on those singular words, creating actual lines of dialogue:

Benjamin: "Ready, Jordan, for a conversation?"
Jordan: "Sure thing, Benjamin, that's prime stimulation!"
Benjamin: "But here's the situation –"
Jordan: "What situation? Darn it, will this be about education?"
Benjamin: "Only if you contribute, and there will be participation!"

Jordan: "Ugh, forget about it – I want my emancipation!"

You'll find it's a fun exercise, because it'll train your brain to find the most melodious words to go with *any* conversation. The flexibility of this exercise is that you can, indeed, do this on your own – you don't need a partner. But just imagine how much more fun this would be with one.

The exercise isn't simply meant to train on rhyme. In fact, I'd wager to say that it trains your ability to improvise and to be as organic as possible with your words.

We're at heart very interactive creatures. We thrive on dialogue, conversation, the back-and-forth. Our brains are *always* used to hearing our own voices, but when we hear *someone else's* voice? That's where the magic happens.

When you force yourself to separate *yourself* into two different characters manifested in your right and left hands, you're instantly creating a situation where you can be on the outside looking in. The lines become very actionable, interactive, *real*. That's where songwriting reaches a new level.

Practice this for twenty minutes a day. What you'll find are true gems in couplets that were meant to be together in a song.

Exercise #2: "Word Tennis"

You know how it works: two players and a net between both on a square court. They bounce a ball back and forth in the hopes of outdoing the other. Sometimes it's totally hypnotic, watching that darn ball go *back and forth, back and forth, back and forth*.

But maybe you're just not into tennis. It honestly depends on the players.

This exercise takes the idea and turns it into a word exercise of a similar style and vision.

Imagine a tennis court:

On one side will be a list of nouns related to a specific field, industry, profession, situation, or concept. Write them in with a pencil: you might include anything like a *hose, dalmatian, truck,* or *siren* if your chosen topic would be the *fire department*, as an example. The more nouns you can include, the better, but perhaps no more than ten.

On the *other* side of the tennis court, list out a set of verbs that are *completely* unrelated.

Here's the deal with *Word Tennis* before I move forward: you *can* decide to go with a list of verbs that are related to the *fire department* and have the nouns be unrelated. Flexibility is key. There are *no* wrong answers here with this exercise. Even if what you've created based on this Word Tennis exercise is sheer crappy drivel, the point of the exercise is to loosen up your mind and cultivate some creative ideas that may spur you into writing a composition that's worth publishing.

Once you have both sides of the tennis court completed with nouns and verbs, start 'bouncing' your 'tennis ball' back and forth from noun to verb (or verb to noun) until you have every word connected. The result will guide you in how to think of the composition of your song based on those words.

The verbs (or nouns) you choose can be anything. In the current example, we'll choose four verbs to go with our four nouns:

- Hose
- Dalmatian
- Truck
- Siren

- Vilify
- Slap
- Annihilate
- Sing

Now I picked those four verbs out of the blue without thinking of the nouns. That's the point of Word Tennis. You have no idea where the 'ball' is going to go.

Start with *hose* and draw a line to any one of these verbs. Doesn't matter which. You can then draw *another* line from the verb to another noun of your choice. From there, draw a line back to another verb that wasn't chosen – and so on and so forth, until all words have been linked.

What you have may just be a truly nonsensical splash or puree of the bizarre, reminding you of why we have natural order in this world. But that's *entirely* the point.

My hose sings songs
Like sirens slapping Dalmatians
To annihilate trucks

...*what?* Come again? That's right: I just wrote the strangest limerick in history by playing Word Tennis, and wouldn't you know it... these three lines alone do something profound:

They get your attention, don't they?

Now don't get me wrong, chances are pretty good these three lines will *never* get to see the white of a paper for someone to sing, but that's okay. The lines developed from playing Word

Tennis really aren't *intended* to be part of a real song (although they *could* be if you so choose).

The point of the exercise is to just break your brain out of the habit of thinking logically with language. Poetry, if not song-writing, is anything *but* logic. It's more emotional. Visual. Actionable. And it may not make sense at first, but if you do read in between these lines, you might resonate with something on how it makes you feel.

Maybe the 'hose' is your mouth, singing the songs so hard that they're like those sirens out in the ocean, slapping old white men (Dalmatians) in the face with their music, and by doing so, they annihilate the 'trucks' (cargo?) because those sailors weren't paying attention as the ship collided with an... iceberg or something.

The beauty of Word Tennis is that you don't *have* to stop there with the number of nouns and verbs you have. Take a look at what you have, expand further, build on, flesh out, centralize toward a theme that most likely was birthed straight out from how you organized the original words. It *may* be crazy – but that's a good thing. Because it's *original*.

Practice with this daily, and you'll be surprised at how your brain will flow with some of the most creative yarns ever in history. 99% of them will be nuts, of course. But, again, I stress: that's the entire point.

Exercise #3: "Scavenger Hunt"

This might take you back to being a kid for good reason, because who *doesn't* love a great scavenger hunt, right? The energy, the drive, the motivation, the hope, the *finish line* – they're all aspects of a great scavenger hunt, usually littered with riddles, ques-tions, or limericks to get your brain working forward on a journey of discovery – sometimes of the *self*, other times of candy and toys.

This exercise is *sort of* like that. Same idea, though.

Start with just *any* melody in your head. It could be one you like, one you've heard before, or if you're feeling especially creative, a brand-new one. Humming the melody is easy, and it's also easy repeating it over and over again, because that melody is the basis for your song until you hit that bridge, which then amplifies the coming ending.

What you need are the *words* to go with the melody.

Take any ordinary paperback – preferably one that's so old that you won't care if you're highlighting certain words in yellow with a marker. As you're humming, open the book to *any* page – don't think about what page. Just open the book. And start skimming through the lines of the book as you're humming your melody.

What you'll notice is that your brain will be instantly drawn to certain words that *sound* like they might fit into your melody. Don't worry about whether the words relate to each other. Just go with it.

You'll highlight maybe ten or more words, and from there, choose *one* to be what we'll call the *anchor*. That word, whatever it may be, will encompass the entire theme of your song. Your job from there will then be to link all other words you've highlighted to your *anchor*.

Do this on a piece of paper:

- Draw a circle
- Write the *anchor* inside of it
- Branch out lines to each other word you've highlighted

Now by branching out to those other words, you're going to

be thinking of how those words might *relate* to the anchor. It may be a stretch, or it may not. Who knows. The point is to get your brain to really *think* about the possibilities.

What's great about this exercise is the flexibility: there are no rules, per se. However your brain will work, that's how it will go. For the most part, each word may represent a single line in your composition. You can then ask yourself the simple questions:

- Should each line rhyme?
- How long should each line be?
- Will the *anchor* be my song title?

You can even combine a couple of words into a phrase as a focus or just as an idea that's branched from the anchor. Whatever works for you as long as you realize that the single word(s) represents a standalone 'clue' or 'treasure' or 'symbol' of progression:

You're essentially *getting to the end of your journey in discovering a song*. The scavenger hunt's final treasure at the end where "X marks the spot" is, in fact, your completed song.

Like with the previous exercise, don't expect to create a Grammy winner with this. But inspiration fuels a masterpiece. And the more you do this, the better chance of not only creating something rather workable, but perhaps *really* infectious to the ears.

The point to always remember with this exercise is that it's the *push*. Think of it as being on a bike with training wheels, and you're just learning. All you need is that *push* to get going.

Exercise #4: "Famous Quote Soup"

This one's a fun one to do given the scope of discovery you have. You might need a book of famous quotes, or at least Google to pull up a webpage littered with potentially hundreds of interesting sayings. Here's seven of them for your perusal:

1. "The greatest glory in living lies not in never falling, but in rising every time we fall." – *Nelson Mandela*
2. "The way to get started is to quit talking and begin doing." – *Walt Disney*
3. "Your time is limited, so don't waste it living someone else's life. Don't be trapped by dogma – which is living with the results of other people's thinking." – *Steve Jobs*
4. "If life were predictable, it would cease to be life and be without flavor." – *Eleanor Roosevelt*
5. "If you look at what you have in life, you'll always have more. If you look at what you don't have in life, you'll never have enough." – *Oprah Winfrey*
6. "If you set your goals ridiculously high and it's a failure, you will fail above everyone else's success." – *James Cameron*
7. "Life is what happens when you're busy making other plans." – *John Lennon*

I found these in less than ten seconds online with just one Google search. No joke. Just looking at these seven quotes brings up a plethora of visuals ripe for development in a composition. But don't use *all* that you see here, because that honestly would be considered plagiarism.

Rather *analyze* each and every quote. Highlight two, maybe three words, for each one. In this example, here's what *I* will highlight:

- *The greatest glory*
- *quit talking*

- *begin doing*
- *time is limited*
- *trapped by dogma*
- *cease to be life*
- *be without flavor*
- *always have more*
- *never have enough*
- *set your goals ridiculously high*
- *Life is what happens*

What would work best in this case is to have each of these snippets written out on a strip of paper...

Now that you've done that... start *organizing*!

That means to move those strips around, trying to see where this song can start, progress, and then maybe *end*. Chances are this may only be the chorus or a verse. Whatever the case may be, this also *propels* you to something profound, essentially *stealing* from the most infamous of quotes in history to conjure up something that's perhaps twisted to some degree.

Just from looking at these snippets, I could easily write it out as:

*Greatest glory's to **quit talking** and **begin doing** –*
***Time's limited** as your coffee's brewing.*
***Trapped by dogma**, you'll **cease to be life** –*
*All **without flavor** to savor that you'll **always have more**,*
*Saying you'll **never have enough**.*
*Because **life is what happens** as your **goals get set***
***ridiculously high** –*
And then you realize, this is the best that will happen –
Time just flies by.

Sparky. Snazzy. Witty.

It certainly helps that the quotes I collected all speak to a common main idea. This little 'poem' may or may not make it as a song, but it certainly ignited a language that's potentially ripe for a song with a little bit of tweaking and cutting of filler words, especially if you already have a melody in your mind.

Case in point, I developed that literally within a minute. That was just from deriving short nuggets from rather memorable quotes spoken by the most famous of people.

Obviously, as you look at your snippets, you'll want to make connections, bridging the words in ways that are conducive to rhyme and rhythm. The beauty of this exercise is that you just made it that much easier on yourself to expand on what you had collected with words so profoundly musical and poetic in nature – such as "greatest glory" or "trapped by dogma". The abstract nature of these snippets lends itself to the evolution of what's written – into something that can actually be *expressed* through music.

Exercise #5: "Pump Up the Metaphor Jam"

You're not alone if you have issues with metaphors (or similes, for that matter). They're not standard in language today. We don't go around comparing things to other things as a way of describing them. We tend to be more linear than that.

Songwriting, however, offers you the ability to draw a listener in and become an interacting member of a visual. That's why metaphors work in them so well.

This exercise will tighten up that device for you, *pumping it up* as it were to ensure you have a rich vocab ripe with visuals to discover in a language with layers and layers of meaning.

Here's how the exercise works: let's start with the word 'shoes'.

Visualize it. Hold that image in your head. Got it? Good. Here's what you're going to do with that word in your head:

- Find at least three unique metaphors for the word 'shoes'
- Describe those three metaphors, exploring the imagery in detail
- Then come up with a really cool line for each

Don't beat yourself up if this one's hard, because remember: you're working with metaphors, the rocket launchers of creative English if you think about it (in fact, the comparison to 'rocket launchers' is a metaphor, too).

So here's a layout of how the word 'shoes' would work out:

- *He lives in a **shoe**. He takes his home with him, wearing his **shoes**. His home is a **shoe**. He lives out of his **shoe**. Welcome **shoe**.*
- *She's a **shoe-in** (shoo-in). Something that's guaranteed. Definite. Obvious choice. The **shoe** gets in to hold the door open. No **shoe**-out, only in.*
- *You've been **shoed**. You've been fitted with something. Equipped. Maintained. Get **shoed**.*

Exercise #6: "Reverse Charades"

As a rule, charades often plays off the fact that you *can't* know what the object, theme, thing, place, person, or concept is. Instead, you have to guess it within a time limit. Many find the game to be so fun that variations have been created, and still to this day the activity reigns supreme in family homes.

This exercise flips it. Kind of.

You're correct if you're thinking that this one's going to be enjoyable as well (come to think of it, *all* of these exercises are enjoyable). It *is* slightly based on the infamous game except you're the only one playing. And instead of trying to guess the 'object', you're trying to come up with ideas that actually describe it, and also only in writing! Hence why it's called *Reverse Charades*.

Let's take the word 'pineapples', for instance:

The way the exercise works is that you *must* use *all* your five senses in describing the word:

1. See
2. Hear
3. Taste
4. Touch
5. Smell

Get a pen and paper ready. Like the game, you're going to give yourself a time limit. When you're ready, you *must* write completely and *freely*, without form. Ensure one particular description utilizes all five senses in some way. Disregard grammar rules, punctuation, syntax, and more. Write *fast*. Think *fast*. And generate *as many words as you can about the word*.

This exercise could conceivably be played as a real reverse version of Charades, too, but with specific rules: how many words you generate will matter, how abstract it is will matter, how *creative* the descriptions are will most *definitely* matter!

The point of the exercise is to not even tell a story. Simply sketch a visual of what the object is within ten minutes. Just let it all go – let the pen (or pencil) move. Write whatever comes to mind based on what the object is – in this case, pineapple – and see what you come up with.

Those are the only rules. You don't need to write something

specific about pineapples. You can write about *anything* that may be related to pineapples.

If it makes you think of the ocean or even Hawaii, write about it. Write about beaches, hula hoops, leis, and ukuleles if you want. This exercise is all about no holds barred, free-for-all, so have at it.

What does this exercise strengthen? Your ability to describe things in writing *creatively*.

Now I *did* say ten minutes, and I mean that *exactly*. Don't go over that time limit. In fact, you'll probably feel the urge to keep going, but resist it. Psychologically, the richest images that come to mind often come first and fresh as you're writing, but if you let it linger too long, the building blocks of your creative imagination may begin to stagnate.

Think of yourself as an architect, and your job is to make a building. You want it to be as simple and clean in style as possible (unless you're from the Renaissance or something), but the more you embellish the design, building upon the initial framework, you tend to muddle the overall aspect of it.

The thoughts then become cluttered. Convoluted. Overwritten. That's the point of the ten minutes.

Now the exercise may be tricky, but here's the beauty of it: there's no scale with 10 being the best and 1 being the worst. Just dismiss yourself into this new world of creation and have fun. An example of working this exercise on the word 'pineapple' may go like this:

Fresh gold ridges, planted from the Earth, bright, juicy, cut, slice to the core, opening a treasure with pleasure to discover tart gems to pop in the mouth for nourishment on an island filled with palm trees, sipping on Mai Tais and reveling in the joy and splendor of God's creation, plentiful, but when I touch you it hurts, the breeze on the beach, golden hour, the sun on your face, Brazilian carnival headdress, finding the value in using strength to reach, my mom's pineapple mousse, break down, relishing in the juice to hydrate underneath the sun, pure hydration, carving the goodness out, like a sculptor, shaving pieces off taking time to enjoy every single bite, feeling the heat of a summer afternoon, hearty, hot, paired with the grounded and soft succulence of coconut, combining the sun and moon together for completion in a life already with a cup running over with blessings.

The beauty of this is within the matrix of this excerpt may very well be a *song*!

Taking what you've written, refining the lines, targeting the theme based on the image – these are the nuts and bolts of songwriting, and now you have the materials needed to make this 'building' as an architect would. The bones are there. The construct is ready. You'll then see how the foundation will hold up with what you have.

Remember: *free-write*. Generally, you'll most likely go for at least 100 words. The more, the better. Don't try to write a story or anything. The exercise is meant to be about as abstract as possible, focusing on your senses – what you're seeing, smelling, tasting, touching, and hearing.

If your main language, by the way, isn't English, that's okay – this isn't an exercise on the English language. If it's Spanish, write it in Spanish. If it's German, write it in German. If it's Portuguese, definitely write it in Portuguese.

Exercise #7: "The Eavesdropper"

If you've used your phone's voice memos app to record every-thing the professor says during class, then this one's a no-brainer. All you need is your phone and at *least* two people talking in conversation.

Chances are good you'll have to let the conversants know you're recording them for purposes of songwriting, but that's okay; most likely they'll be fine with that, especially if you're seeking to nurture your creativity.

I know what you're thinking... *that's stupid and pointless.* No, it's not. On the surface, it is. Underneath it all, you have the richest repository of dialogue and idiomatic language at your disposal just by pressing 'record' – hence why this may arguably be the easiest exercise for you.

The fact is that you'll have a copy of *interaction* filled to the brim with action words, thoughts then reacted to by others in a conversation, which can turn any song into more than just manu-factured words one after the other – you'll have a true *story* – *communicated* – and *shown* instead of 'told' to those who will listen.

Any storyteller will tell you that dialogue often propels a story like little nitro boosters, but here's a case where you don't necessarily have to explain *anything*. Remember: you're not a story writer – you're a *songwriter*. You don't have to *narrate* here, or explain *anything*.

All you're doing is painting a picture. Dialogue does that better than anything else. One entire conversation can have a simple point behind it that is truly self-made for a song, without having to go through any exposition or "drive the point in" with a needless hammer.

Even in poetry, the beating-a-dead-horse syndrome ends up being a no-no as you just want the visual, the image, to stand on its own and communicate *truth*. That's all you need. That's all you want. Nothing more.

So what's better than simply recording a conversation? *Making that conversation your own.*

- Pick and choose your lines
- Leave all 'asides' behind to trim the fat
- Go for the lean cuts, targeting your most concrete ideas

You want the song based on the conversation you recorded to be aligned with the rhythm you've set for the composition. You're going to *have* to streamline, ultimately instilling a sense of interaction between the singer and the listener.

In other words... you will have hit the jackpot with a song like that.

Exercise #8: "The Personifier"

We may have something trickier here – unless you have the lyrics to work off of (which shouldn't be too hard with the internet around). *This* exercise, contrary to the name, isn't about giving human characteristics to inanimate objects at all. Rather, instead, you're *personifying* your favorite artist.

You do this by nabbing an entire page of lyrics of one song from any of your favorites: it could be Jill Scott, J. Cole, Gregory Porter, or whoever. It most likely should be a song you really like.

Such as Mariah Carey's "Anytime You Need a Friend".

What if her theme wasn't about a 'friend'? What if it was about *mac and cheese* or something? Maybe you're craving a creamy homemade baked mac and cheese (instead of *heartache* as Carey's original focuses on). The goal here is to change the words, *using* Mariah Carey's 'voice' with the composition.

You want to train yourself to create something *original* based on her format. Her style. Her pacing. Her rhythm. Everything. You may notice that it'll be easy given her linear focus with every verse focusing on four lines with eight 'beats' (syllables) for each.

Try even playing instrumental versions of songs, nurturing creativity in developing your own lyrics. Chances are your own creations, though, will be 'throwaways,' but that's okay. Chances are good that a song about *mac and cheese* won't be one you want to be recorded.

In general, this exercise is actually quite fun to work with. It gets you familiar with common structures you'll find with the greats in the music industry. Examine multiple tempos, too, and how the lyrics work with them. Who knows? You might surprise yourself and find something interesting to sing.

Exercise #9: "Tovy-Turpsy"

You've heard of that fun word, right? *Topsy-turvy*. Look it up. It actually is in the dictionary, but you then get to wonder where such a word came from. It certainly didn't have any Greek derivations, nor was it a descendant from a Latin root word. It begs the question: where do some of these weird words come from?

Look up the word *flibbertigibbet*. It'll blow your mind.

The fact is new words have been invented for centuries. It doesn't have to have a literary origin for it to be accepted. Charles Dickens, in fact, came up with the word "boredom". Sylvia Plath thought of the rather ethereal term "dreamscape". And don't even get me started with William Shakespeare:

- Bandit

- Swagger
- Gossip

More than a thousand other words were all created by the Bard himself long after the English language was ever actually a 'thing' you could learn as a language.

So why can't *you* invent words? You *should*.

That's why this exercise is named what it is: it dares to be inventive, creating and twisting something that's well-known into an innovation. It's often called wordplay, which many poets mess with. But as a songwriter, you can focus on these steps to an exercise designed to stretch your literary muscles to the limit.

First, make four lists of roughly a dozen words each. You'll have a list for nouns, a list for adjectives, a list for verbs, and a list for suffixes and prefixes (suffix/prefix examples include 'non-', 'anti-', '-er').

Don't limit yourself to the possibilities. Go with *any* kind of list for each type, and then when you feel you have everything you need, start playing around with them.

1. Nouns

- Bicycle
- Mucus
- Diadem
- Cathedral
- Catheter
- Fulcrum
- Gasoline
- Mirror
- Bulldozer
- Paper
- Wax

- Firewall

2. Adjectives

- Subliminal
- Fiery
- Agonizing
- Feverish
- Simple
- Blackened
- Lovely
- Lax
- Watered
- Breakable
- Solemn
- Saturated

3. Verbs

- Coagulate
- Germinate
- Sweeten
- Sift
- Crack
- Loft
- Enliven
- Investigate
- Plan
- Brown

- Build
- Gallop

4. Suffixes/Prefixes

- de-
- -able
- non-
- -ness
- im-
- -ful
- ex-
- -y
- un-
- -est
- mis-
- -ible

The fun then begins. You can easily combine *mirror* with a suffix like *-ful* to get "mirrorful" to describe a room of mirrors or a hall of mirrors.

Combine *any* two items on any of these lists and get something like "paperwax" (which there is no such thing in this world called 'paperwax'). But the *image* will then be firmly planted in your head as to *how* to describe what *paperwax* is.

You can use an adjective as an adverb with a verb and say something like "lofting lax" and *still* know what it means even if it's not technically grammatically correct. What you've done is not only create a new 'phrase' but make it sound musical, lyrical, and alliteral (remember that poetic device?).

The sky's the limit with this exercise as you can come up with all sorts of phrases that will mean something to *you* and then give you creative license to subtly explain it in a song or poem. The creations will catch the eye and at first make a reader or listener beg the question as to *what the heck that word was*. Then again, that's what many thought of William Shakespeare when he came up with the word 'multitudinous' (derived from 'multitude').

(That word simply means the same as... *'a lot'*.)

Exercise #10: "The Mirrorizer"

Taking a cue from the last exercise, this one's named via obvious wordplay, albeit understandable when you dig deep into the meaning: it's about being a 'mirror' for your own work, but then discovering something within the 'reflection' that might work *better* or *different* than the original.

Might be too many metaphors there, but the good news is you're seeing even *more* examples of how these poetic devices work!

In a nutshell, here's how the *mirrorizer* exercise works:

1. Take any song you've created, preferably on your computer or phone.
2. Highlight all adjectives, adverbs, and nouns in the song.
3. Then copy all the adjectives, adverbs, and nouns into one list.
4. Look up each word in a thesaurus and list the most *interesting* synonyms.

5. Then *copy* your original song, substituting the synonyms.

You might be surprised to know how interesting the results would be. You could even do this with a relatively well-known song and discover some *real* golden nuggets with this exercise.

It's important to put away the original work and the newly created work for a couple of days, so you can look at the comparison with fresh eyes. Here's what you might be asking yourself as you look at both versions:

- *Did I change the meaning with these new synonyms?*
- *Has the rhythm, flow, or sound changed (good or bad)?*
- *Do any of these new synonyms have multiple meanings (which can be a good thing)?*
- *And lastly, does this actually improve the composition of the song?*

The reality is this may just improve your composition dramatically as you never thought of using the word *seething* in place of *fuming*, for example, in a song about rage. One substitution could change the entire makeup of a song, for better or worse. Ultimately, the final benefit you get from participating in this exercise is that you receive an even deeper understanding of how the language works for you in your songwriting.

You could, in fact, go through this exercise with a well-known song from a musical artist in the industry. How about Alicia Keys' "If I Ain't Got You"?

You might go from the first verse and pre-chorus in the song:

Some people live for the fortune
Some people live just for the fame

Some people live for the power, yeah
Some people live just to play the game

Some people think
That the physical things
Define what's within
And I've been there before
That life's a bore
So full of the superficial

To...

Someone may live for the money
Someone may live just for the Gram
Someone may live for the system, yeah
Someone may live just to fool their heart

Some may believe
That the things we can touch
Describe what's inside
And I've been witness
That living's a road
So filled of apparent things

The weird and scary thing is the 'revision' of Alicia Keys' iconic hit *actually* sounds decent with the right tempo and rhythm in place. I'd personally go with the original, but you can see what synonyms do to the meaning, voice, and overall *style* of a song.

That's how you 'mirrorize' an original song – you're creating a reflection, but also *different* in a way.

The possibilities are endless with these exercises as your lyrics flourish. The question then you have to ask is... what about the *music*?

PART III

8

FINDING YOUR UNIQUE 'VOICE' AMONG MANY VOICES

"The only art I'll ever study is stuff that I can steal from."

—David Bowie

I simply cannot stress enough that *anything* you hear on the radio or on your playlist is, in fact, *not* original. Not *truly* original, anyway. It doesn't matter how talented you really are; everything you create will always be based on your previous knowledge and experience.

So don't fret. As an artist, you're a *collector*. In fact, the great Jonathan Lethem once said that even when you call something 'original', nine times out of ten you probably don't even know the references or original sources.

You might feel like you're 'stealing' a melody or a hook, but what you're going to learn right here is how you can make what already exists into *your own* via your personal touch. Reinvention. Revamping. Reinvigorating. The heart of the music industry is in honoring what's come before you and providing a *new* way to appreciate what's been done.

Bear in mind this important fact, though: there's a fine line between 'stealing' (I use the term loosely, but as you can see, David Bowie didn't seem to have a problem with it) and *plagiarizing*.

Let's first define what originality really is.

Here's Merriam-Webster's take on it:

"The quality or state of being original."

The first thought you'll have based solely on that is... "Okay, what does that mean???"

I'm sure you've experienced this on many occasions when the dictionary 'stumbles' or 'fumbles' around a definition due to the meaning being rather abstract. Such definitions are hard to pinpoint an exact meaning that's capable of being articulated or explained, but here's the good news: you can go *further* with it:

Merriam-Webster then defines the term 'original' (instead of 'originality') as:

"Independent and creative in thought or action."

Okay... that's better. Still, it gets a bit more complicated as we end up diving a bit into some philosophy. Can I *truly* be independent and creative in thought and action, knowing that:

- I'm a social being derived from interactions with other people?
- I'm also defined by their ideas, thoughts, and influence?
- There's almost *no* room for true innovation at all!

After all, music has been around since the beginning of time. By now it would be hard to come up with something... *truly* original. Right?

Your first step in this whole originality thing is to accept and understand that *nothing* you write will *truly* be original at all. That's part of being a good artist, in fact. *Creative* originality – not *true* originality – comes from injecting a fresh new perspective on something you already know, something that was most likely created by somebody else.

Okay, so what about plagiarism? Everyone talks about plagiarism!

And they should. Sadly sometimes it's very difficult seeing that fine line between 'inspiration' and 'plagiarism'. Sure, Bowie called it 'stealing', but that's not to say he would claim what he stole was actually *his*. The music industry's funny like that... Go ahead and steal a motif or guitar riff if you like, but if you walk around claiming *you* were the one who created that style, motif, concept, or masterpiece of a musical device, chances are good you'll be charged with plagiarism.

In short, if someone can *easily* spot a section of your composition that has undeniably been pulled from someone else's work *without question*, that is considered plagiarism.

There's no denying it. This then begs the obvious question: *how can I be inspired, building on what I know from previous music artists, without plagiarizing?*

Many may not like the answer, but you're *not* intending for it to be the case... It's simply by noticing that *your* creation isn't 'detectable'!

Let's put that in perspective, though.

You're not *trying* to hide anything. The intention matters a lot in this case. As a creator, you want creations to come *solely* from you – when you take a previous idea, you're taking it not for the easy route in completing a composition.

You're taking that idea as *inspiration* – which invites immediate change, experimentation, and invention.

Let's add more specifics here when trying to visualize that 'fine line'. Consider academic writing, for instance, and what the difference may be between 'paraphrasing' and 'plagiarizing'. Asking these questions may shed some light on the issue for you:

1. What is my song structure compared to?
2. Am I changing keys with my hook and chorus?
3. How long am I taking from the first verse to the pre-chorus?
4. Am I using interesting chord variations?
5. Am I using a different pitch and tone?
6. Are my progressions in a different 'order' than the source I'm 'copying' from?

Take Alicia Keys "If I Ain't Got You" and compare her song to my changed copy of it and ask yourself this important question:

*Without even hearing the melody... would **you** be able to tell that **my** copy was **stolen** from Alicia Keys?*

In my opinion... it wouldn't be the first thing that would come to mind at all.

Paraphrasing is when you, in fact, liberally *use synonyms* to replace all sorts of important words in the copied work. Changing up the sentence structure plenty also contributes to ensuring you're not plagiarizing. Even mixing the order of lines around makes it very clear that you're, in fact, paraphrasing.

I would probably have to experiment with the melody, trying different chord progressions within the same meter and pace, because *if* I were to use the same hook, the same *sound* of the song Keys created, that would be the equivalent of setting myself in hot water with the music industry. No doubt, if I make changes to the lyrics, chances are good I also *must* make changes to the music.

It is the very *definition* of taking something that was created by someone else and making it *completely your own*.

Mastering the art of 'listening' and 'collecting'.

Perhaps you're very much into piano. If so, bravo. I am too. It's *really* easy strumming one chord progression on a piano. All you need are your fingers. Even better – you can hum it, especially if you've pinpointed the progression with your own voice. But oftentimes the piano is a catalyst for being able to hear what works and what doesn't work.

You learn this by picking out the songs you love, looking up those chords. You then learn how to play them. But the idea of playing them isn't just to practice your skills, but to understand what progressions *actually* work together quite well.

Who knows? Your strumming might result in discovering unexpected chord progressions that actually do sound quite pleasing to the ear, but were never explored by the original artist. It doesn't mean that the artist 'missed something', of course. The reason for choosing the actual chord progression when there might've been something even *nicer* in style may have simply been a stylistic choice.

Finding those specific 'golden nuggets' in distinct chord progressions that are obvious derivations of original sequences can then be massive sources of inspiration. Let that drive your creation forward as a songwriter. You'll be surprised at what you might discover, empowered to play around further with what you know *without* fear of plagiarism.

Beware this 'vicious cycle', though.

Let's call it the 'waiting game'.

If we're singers, we often get scared that we might sound like *Justin Bieber* or *Ed Sheeran*, which automatically pegs us as useless carbon copies. The fear is understandable, but comparisons are unavoidable.

You have to remember: we're all complex beings defined by those around us, our cultures, our experiences, our past. Ultimately, how you sound *will* remind others of past musicians before you.

Instead of waiting to find your 'unique voice' before getting started... simply *get started* to discover *exactly* who you are *freely*. Experiment. Commit trial and error. Fail. Succeed. Flesh your voice out until you understand it fully.

The fact is you'll instantly see your inspirations in your own voice, no doubt, but you'll *also* see that there's creation in that voice that makes it your *own*. It's you. It's *not* Bieber. It's *not* Sheeran.

It's all *you*.

Paul McCartney said in a BBC interview about how inspiring some American artists were to the Beatles early in their career: "in our minds, we were just copying it... but when you copy a thing, you're never like them. You're your own thing."

The challenge is in beating this Catch-22 – in that, if we don't hang on to our sources of inspiration, we'll struggle in finding our own 'voices', and if we *do* hang on to our sources of inspiration too much, we'll end up sounding *too* much like somebody else. It's a tricky balance.

So don't stress about the 'balance'. Reach for the unknown creative territory instead. You might as well fail when trying to find your own voice. Stop judging yourself. Don't worry about getting out of your comfort zone as you start wondering whether or not you sound like D'Angelo or Janet Jackson or whatever. That will be your foundation.

When you feel you've hit that *recognition* in a voice that clearly represents your *strength* – your *desire* to express emotion – you can then expand on it and make it your own in creative ways if you so choose.

In fact, chances are you *must* choose. Choose to be *you*. Choose to be the *creative* you.

9

THOU SHALT NOT JUDGE YOUR OWN MUSIC

"I was washing dishes at the Greyhound bus station at the time and I said, 'Awap bop a lup bop a wop bam boom, take 'em out!'."

—Little Richard

Ever heard the phrase, "You are your worst critic"? That couldn't be truer anywhere else.

There's no question that *every* musician in existence has at one point or another doubted inner talent, thinking it was a futile cause – this theory of being a *songwriter*, an *artist*, a true visionary of the music industry. What separates the greats from those who fall away is that while you might struggle with it, you definitely don't let it *become* all that you are.

That's why songwriting is a *constant* in your life. You're *always* going to be writing. It's to fend off the doubt every day before those weeds take root and kill the nutrition of your creative mind. If you *don't* write all the time – and if it's *because* you doubt your talent – you most definitely will 'die' *without* your talent.

Take Little Richard, for instance, and his quote at the beginning of the chapter.

He's not exaggerating at all. Imagine what would happen if he had passed *too* much judgment on something as 'silly' as "awap bop a lup bop a wop bam boom" while washing some dishes – we most likely would *not* have the foundation for an entire genre from *the innovator, the originator, and the architect of Rock and Roll* himself. Not to mention that his music also helped shape R&B for generations!

Little Richard did *not* doubt himself at all. He might've thought how quirky it was that he was singing while messing with soapy water at a grungy bus station, but little did he know he had hit a goldmine, and it was his inner *talent* that made those unique lyrics work.

Case in point, don't be your worst critic. Don't be *any* critic, in fact. Embrace imperfection. It's challenging since your brain *wants* perfection, but what you need to do is resist it with all your will.

Just because it sounds 'weird' doesn't mean it isn't *good*. Sometimes we don't realize we're looking at treasure – sometimes those 'golden nuggets' look like nothing more than rocks.

Here's a trick in tricking your mind into thinking those 'rocks' are actually *golden nuggets*.

Improvise.

I'll give you the benefit of the doubt on many occasions here. Sometimes you just don't have the time. Or even the strength. Sometimes life *really* does get in the way. You get so burdened by the troubles that you almost certainly will pass judgment on yourself, crumpling up that paper with a few words of lyrics written in – without even considering that it *might* be something unique and interesting.

So this is what you do: you *improvise*.

What I mean by that is *forcing* yourself to just make something. *Anything*. Don't worry about its value or how bad it might be. Just go ahead and create it. Who cares? This is the basis of the 'throwaways,' in fact. Alicia Keys endorses that free flow, stating that "improvisation plays a really big role in the songwriting process, just being open, just being fluid."

This is the case where it's not about the goal of actually writing a song.

It's about getting your mind free of the doubt that you *can't* write that song. The actual *act* of writing can destroy that doubt with ease, *proving* that you actually *can* do it. You never know unless you try. In fact, it might even help you realize more of your strengths as a poetic artist.

This holds hands with *really* getting yourself out of your comfort zone.

Stretch your limits. Remember: this is like working out. Your voice, your music, they're like *muscles*. You're going to want to work them – sometimes quite hard.

Here are some things you can do to challenge yourself:

- Start writing the bridge of the song first (instead of the chorus or verse)
- Change the melody you've chosen to a different tune or tone
- Try a few normal chord changes until you find something you like

- Try a different instrument – like a kazoo, or mandolin, or... a tambourine!

Be just... *weird*. Maybe bizarre. Go off the wall with ways to create the music. Think of Michael Jackson and how "Don't Stop 'Til You Get Enough" employed the use of percussion from... *glass water bottles*? Yes, that's really a thing – at least for Sheila E.

Music exists everywhere. Discover something new. It's the discovery that matters, not what you discover. After all, 99% of the time, what you discover might just be a 'throwaway,' and guess what: that's okay.

10

FIND THE PATTERN TO YOUR MELODIES

"Lyrics can be important, but ultimately, what pulls people in on a song is melody and the tracks and the way the music feels."

—Babyface

Everything has a pattern – whether it's in nature, or in the latest single from The Weeknd. If you listen closely, you'll hear it – it may be in a motif that's consistently repeated, or it may be in a vocal stamp, like how Prince used to do it in his music. We hear it everywhere. We just don't hear it *as* music (at least not yet). Therefore, there is no right or wrong way to find your melody. It's simply *out there*. You already learned that you *can* choose it – here's *how*.

It's the truth that you can be a part of any genre of music out there: Hip-Hop, R&B, Pop, Alternative, Country, Gospel, Jazz, Classical. It doesn't matter. *Every* sound you've heard was derived from the sounds of nature or *something else*. This is often why the best melodies often hit a musician when they're doing something else – when the senses are at their most optimal.

In fact, anyone's *voice* while speaking is ripe pickings for a melody when you hear inflection. Perhaps the sound of the ocean in its rhythmic spark can inspire a song. Chris Stapleton once said, "The curse of being a songwriter is that you're always at work. I could look out the window right now and see something that would make me want to write."

Knowing that a melody is out there that might be related to something already created won't matter. You might discover that melody in a *different way* than how it was originally created by a previous artist, and *that* alone makes it your own. But sometimes you'll need a little direction in what *kind* of melody you want to embrace for your song:

1. Happy songs will mainly dominate in a major key.
2. Sad songs will mainly focus on a minor key.
3. Being creative with lyrics and mood juxtaposition might open up new inventions.
4. Or you can be ambitious: use *both* major and minor keys in your melody.

Whatever tactic you try to employ, make sure you do this one thing: the melody you create *has* to relate to some form of nature listeners can identify with to some degree. That gives you remarkable license to open up the expanse of creativity beyond what's been done or heard before.

Now the question is: how do I move from format to sound?

One of the bigger challenges most songwriters have is matching the sound to the lyrics. It can be a painstaking process. After all, you'd be hard-pressed to find a melody that matches Shakespeare's 'multitudinous' word with all the syllables piled in.

This is often why shorter, punchier words tend to work much better in lyrics. But it also depends on the genre. You might be in hip-hop where the rhythm really allows you to dictate the ability to incorporate longer, more rhythmic words into your composition, and that can lend itself to a bit more creativity. Slower ballads that are more deliberate and linear often do require much shorter words. So, in short:

Let the rhythm and rhyme of your words match the melody.

How do you make sure your words have rhythm?

Trial and error will go a long way, and many often stumble through this. The key is simply understanding your song *before* you match any words to it: if it's a ballad, stick with shorter words, shorter lines, if it's a peppier piece, you can be more liberal with the length of words and the length of your lines.

More importantly, once you have the melody down pat, simply try singing the song you're currently writing along with the melody just to see if the flow matches. If it does, you've got something going. If it doesn't, back to the drawing board.

It's important to understand that certain lyrics *will* read well... but that doesn't necessarily mean they'll *sing* well. Pay close attention to your pacing as you sing, and if you find yourself constantly tripping over certain words or phrases, you may want to modify those words or lines into something much shorter.

Meter plays a role. Think about Bruno Mars' "That's What I Like". Each and every line had a particular meter to it with exact syllables down to the last count. That's no coincidence. They're designed that way to work with the pace, flow, and rhythm of the song. Add one or two more syllables into that flow, and it may end up sounding too choppy. You'd want to avoid it. There was no doubt Bruno Mars wanted to avoid that as well.

Take notice of how much 'room' there may be for certain words and not enough for others. That may require some balancing out. If the current draft you're working on sports a long word in a line with a bunch of short ones, a melody might sound inconsistent with that. So opt to shorten the long word and elongate the others a bit just to keep it all centered within the overall rhythm of the music.

Likewise, you may notice not enough contrast between sections in the rhythm of the words. This is a case where the opposite is an extreme you want to avoid. You most certainly don't want *every single line* sounding *exactly the same* but with different words, because that lends itself to blandness, boredom, and monotony. Songwriting is anything but.

Instead, have the rhythm – and especially the *rhyme* – control the content, not the other way around. A basic rule of thumb:

If it's fine, perfect rhyme. If it hurts, make it work.

But here's a *real* test: experiment with it through *another* singer. Why? Because *that* singer won't have the benefit of knowing straight out how the lyrics are supposed to go. This gives you an outside-in overview of the strengths and weaknesses of your lyrics, and the recommendations may be eye-opening.

Most of the time, a melody can inspire your lyrics.

There's something so distinct about a melody that perhaps *sounds* like there should be words that go along with it based on the tone, pitch, and overall emotional connotation. If that happens, go with it. That will be a cascade of creativity that won't stop, and you'd even be struggling to come up with an outro to end it all (which sometimes isn't really a bad thing!).

But don't go searching for that golden goose.

You'd be lucky enough to hear a melody in your head that just lures you in, and you can't get it out of your mind. That's a melody begging to be played along with lyrics perfectly matched to it.

Sometimes, you'll just noodle around on the keyboard, guitar, or trombone, stumbling upon a series of notes that just sound harmonious together. If that's the case, great. That can be a hook, your motif, your overall theme of the music, which you can build around with other variations and notes to derive variety from.

Alas, the real truth is that oftentimes the melody inspires you to write the lyrics, defining the theme. Organically, naturally, simply put: it's the perfect way to match your melody with the lyrics.

Putting two and two together.

Once you think you've got a melody down as well as the lyrics, you more often than not will then try to 'fit' them together in a way that's synergistic. Simply singing along won't be enough. *All* of it has to fit.

This may involve some tweaking of the melody to accommodate, but remember this important point: your music should almost always come *first*. When in doubt, tweak the *lyrics* instead. If you can't, *then* focus on the music.

There are some things you can do to work with the lyrics you've created, such as:

- Stretching vowels and vocal sounds to match the music (within reason)

- Omit unnecessary words like "that" and "of"
- Write in active, not passive, voice (passive often requires more syllables)
- Use contractions when necessary to shorten (ex: instead of "could have," go with "could've" or "coulda")
- Add informality and slang

Before you know it, you're actually *enjoying* the editing process, because it will be like discovery for you. Almost like you're picking certain flavors of candy out of a bag of Skittles, and the joy in doing so takes you away to a place where time doesn't exist. It's that joy in constantly working on fixing up a song to match the melody with the lyrics, and then when you're done...

The gratification is utterly glorious. The accomplishment is well worth it.

11

YOU DON'T HAVE TO GO IT ALONE, THOUGH: YOU WILL HAVE TECHNOLOGY!

"Music is not math. It's science. You keep mixing the stuff up until it blows up on you, or it becomes this incredible potion."

—Bruno Mars

Be my guest if you'd like to be the balladeer roaming the earth with guitar in hand and a notebook and pen in a satchel, waiting for the next piece of inspiration to hit. That's the ideal vision of a songwriter, a bard, if you will.

Armed with nothing but the notes and words of your heart, you *press on*. Writer's block? Never heard of it. You never tire of strumming notes, echoing the sounds of nature into your soul the way tea steeps in water, fluidly mixing into sheer paradise. That's how your blood flows, man.

But you can't deny it: technology *does* help. That's really all it *should* do, mind you... but it *is* quite the help in pushing your songwriting to the next level at least somewhat *faster* and maybe even a bit more *accurate*.

Many songwriters struggle with rhyme, for instance.

You're not alone. Perhaps you even struggled through the chapter instructing you on the types of rhyme, and that's okay. We all can't be poets. But we *can* use technology to help us along.

Try out these resources and see what you come up with:

- Chorus (songwriting app)
- The Complete Rhyming Dictionary by Clement Wood
- MasterWriter
- Rhymezone
- Rhymer
- Rhymer's Block

Thanks to the internet, there's a whole host of potential candidates and resources to leverage, so explore. Research to your heart's content. After all, this is what artists do!

You may wonder how the masters did all of it in the past, but when you think about the fact that there are *more* people on this Earth than thousands of years ago, and we all live in a society that moves via super-speed with constant bills to pay, salaries to make, and vacations to take, it makes sense that you want to fast-track as much as possible just to complete songwriting passion projects.

You can also benefit a lot from recording apps as well like:

- Ableton Live Lite
- Audacity
- GarageBand
- Pro Tools First

Here are some video conferencing alternatives when working real-time with other musicians:

- BandLab
- ConnectionOpen
- LANDR Sessions

The best part is that these tools are generally free or have a trial version to use. So barriers, come if you may, but nothing will stop you from writing and recording your best songs. Even from the comfort of your own home.

PART IV

12

SO WHAT ARE YOU WAITING FOR? START RECORDING!

"When I first started recording music,
we would record in the closet with socks on the mic."

—Lil Yachty

Now *that* is the magic place: the recording studio. Many have said that's where the magic happens, but I'd beg to differ. It's a great place to be in, but you have to have had the magic *before* walking into one. Or else you're just singing into a different mic in a soundproof room. Nothing special.

The important thing to remember about recording your music is that you *must* do it. It doesn't matter where: just stop procrastinating and *do it*! Easier said than done, though.

Most of us don't have a built-in recording studio in our apartment. We don't have the resources to lease a building that can be built with a stage, soundproof room, all the bells and whistles, and more to ensure your recording is the *exact* perfection you imagined in your head.

Ever tried recording your voice in the middle of the kitchen?

You'd end up hearing noise that would make you go crazy, and unless you're trying to go for some nostalgic old-school scratchy country record type recording, that's not what you're going for.

You want clean, concise, crisp, collected, crystallized sound in your recordings without letting any listener know that there are *surroundings* around you. Let's be frank here: a listener *knows* that he or she is jamming to a track that was most likely recorded in a studio, but that same listener doesn't want to be constantly reminded of that!

What you need to do is listen to your *own* voice.

Record yourself *first*. Know *how* you sound and *where* you sound. You might have a nook, cranny, or corner in your house that can serve well with serviceable acoustics, and that's fine and dandy. But if you don't at the very least love your voice, it'll show in your recording, and it'll be receptive to listeners as well.

Most of us get shocked at hearing ourselves in a recording. That's natural. The challenge is trying to get past the shock and *still* believe with confidence that what you've recorded is a great work of art, not letting your *voice* get in the way of that.

So here are some interesting tips to overcome that challenge:

- Find that nice-sounding room with decent acoustics (getting into a wardrobe with a comforter around you could do the job as well)
- Be particular about where you place your microphone since you want to have it in the same direction you project your voice
- Experiment with varying vocal processes and recording methods

The room you choose is easy. But where do you place your

microphone? That's an art form. You'd be surprised at how different your voice would sound on recording depending on where the microphone is. Experimenting with it will give you the background and foundation to fall back on regarding the confidence you need to believe that while your voice might sound good to *you*, it can *also* sound good on a recording.

It all depends on how you're being picked up. Simply put... *it's not you!* Don't ever think it is.

Have you ever noticed the doubling techniques, often utilized in hip-hop and R&B, with secondary vocals layered on the background? Perhaps you want to implement a compressor, a reverb, a delay, or an Auto-Tune-style effect like Post Malone or Lil Baby. There are a plethora of plug-ins and effects you can play around with to jazz up the recording creatively beyond that of an unplugged version.

More importantly, you'll want to know the basic recording skills necessary to complete the project in full. After all, you're going to be a combination of any or all of these:

- Artist
- Engineer
- Master Engineer
- Mixer
- Musician
- Producer
- Singer
- Songwriter

That'll be hefty. Break it down on a checklist, though, and you won't have any trouble.

1. Save up to get yourself a new laptop if you don't have a good one yet.

2. Purchase a decent microphone (you can start with a USB one).
3. Go with Digital Audio Workstations like *Pro Tools, Logic Pro, Ableton Live, FL Studio,* or *Cubase.*
4. Buy the best quality studio headphones that you can afford.

Tools like Logic Pro and Ableton Live make it possible to transfer basic music files you've recorded to then work on optimizing and pumping vocals or highlighting instrumentals, bass, or others more.

Mixing and mastering can be a breeze thanks to YouTube tutorials, online courses, and other books on the subject, or by partnering with a specialist who can manage it for you. Don't discount the value of having a professional make it happen – even when recording a simple demo, the value's priceless.

The great news is this: the *more* you hear yourself in a recording you're tweaking, editing, mixing, and mastering, the more you end up liking what you're hearing. And you should. But who knows? Maybe I'll write a book about music and vocal production one day!

Either way, it's your creative work. You *deserve* to love it.

SO WRITER'S BLOCK DOES EXIST? KIND OF.

"Nothing will work unless you do."

—Maya Angelou

Surprise... I know I said that writer's block does *not* exist, but not to the extent that it wouldn't exist for *you*.

The temptation to *want* to believe that someday you *might* end up running dry, out of ideas, is the birthing place of writer's block. If there ever was a nasty phoenix rising from ashes, it would be *writer's block*.

So, yes, indeed – writer's block is a *myth*. Keep telling yourself that as the legendary Dolly Parton has:

> *"I've never been someone who gets writer's block. Writing is just as easy for me now as it was fifty years ago. Of course, there are times that I can write better, have greater focus, but there's never a time when I can't write anything at all."*

Sometimes, though, the world makes it very difficult to just keep saying that, and before you know it, you're struggling. Writer's block materializes out of nowhere, plaguing your mind.

What. Do. You. Do?

First off, what really *causes* writer's block?

Is it you? Or something else?

Most of the time, it *is* you. That's the easiest type of writer's block to break. Maya Angelou said it best with "Nothing will work unless you do." We can follow that up with Pablo Picasso, too, "Inspiration exists, but it has to find you working."

You have to stare at yourself in the mirror and tell yourself to stop making excuses for yourself. Do the work. Grit your teeth. Fight it. Before you know it, you'll break the chain.

What happens, though, when writer's block does *not* come specifically from you?

Here are some other common causes:

- Harsh self-criticism
- Fear of comparison to other writers
- Fear of the workload
- Lack of praise
- Lack of self-motivation

In all fairness, a lot of these do tend to overlap with the source of the chain, which is *you*, but sometimes there are external factors here. You might grit your teeth and fight it all you want, but *still* what you're coming up with ends up lackluster for whatever reason. Stress. Strict deadlines. Bad health. Unfortunate medical accidents or injuries. An assortment of calamities can contribute. And it's not your fault.

But you *can* beat this. I know you can. And there are methods you can focus on to do just that.

Here are some tips to overcome the myth that is writer's block:

- Be imperfect
- Focus on daydreaming
- Free-write (about *anything*, not about songs)
- And, last but not least... try *not* starting at the beginning

What does all that mean? Frame your mind the right way, simply put.

Writing isn't *just* about putting the words on paper, mind you. Sometimes – most of the time, perhaps – your writing happens *inside your head*. A lot of the time, we forget that.

We associate songwriting with the physical act: taking a pen, getting some paper, and writing and recording songs. Sure, that's what it is.

But you wouldn't have been able to do that without the mind that made the music and the words in the first place. Remember what came first.

So dispense with the notion that you *have* to be writing *all* the time to be successful. Surely you'll be writing consistently, no doubt, as that's a common paradigm you've already learned when it comes to successful songwriting. But the fact is this: your work will come from somewhere *before* you write it down – your brain.

Let your brain *work*.

When I say "starting at the beginning", understand that there are no 'rules' when it comes to writing a song. We often think that we start at the beginning: the first verse, or maybe even the chorus. Remember, in the end, there are no rules. There are only *guidelines*. And you're in charge of what guidelines to follow in the creative project you're managing, which can differ from project to project.

That's part of the beauty of songwriting: it's always evolving.

Who knows? You might find more inspiration in the bridge because of its melody. Investigate that. Explore bridges and get excited, because everyone knows that when you're excited, you get inspired, thinking that bridges are *everything*, like Pharrell Williams does, from Stevie Wonder to Adele. When you get inspired, you get motivated. When you get motivated, you get the urge to write. And when you write... you *create*.

It goes without saying that you don't *have* to push through the part that's getting you stuck. A common tactic in breaking through writer's block is to just 'write through it'. That can work. But sometimes it won't. So what do you do? Just go back to your favorite part of the song instead and work from there.

The goal is to inject some inspiration to help push you past the threshold of writer's block.

What if that doesn't work? Then it's time to put some boxing gloves on:

- Start with a section of a song you *know* you're not strong in
- Start a song with a section you *thought* would be the chorus
- Explore a different genre, like Country or Alternative (if you're more into, you know, ballads or something)

The trick is to trip yourself up enough to shake you out of the shackles. Be daring. Ambitious. Even risky. Push your mind to a level you didn't expect *just* to see what your brain does. You'd be surprised to then suddenly hit a spark where you can move forward if you adjust some structures and perhaps focus on something uniquely different, something you're not accustomed to.

The good news is that any of this may not work *right away*, and that's okay, because you can always do the tried-and-true method of just taking a break. Let your brain rest. You *have* to remember that songwriting is a craft requiring every ounce of creativity in that mess of neurons in your head. It's not easy.

You need to take care of yourself. Exercise. Go for a walk. Enjoy a bowl of ice cream. Go out with friends. Live life. Walk your dog. Dress like a ninja and walk around like you're trying to hide behind bushes.

Sleep. A lot.

Dream. A lot.

Don't let that crazy thing called a 'deadline' rule you, because in the sense that you're a songwriter and you're only perhaps getting started, you have an advantage here: you have *no deadlines*. So don't worry about it.

You *can* take a break from all of it. Sometimes you can just move on to a different idea to make into a song, and you might find even more inspiration that way. In the end, once you come back to the stumbling block, whatever it is, you'll come back fresh with new eyes and most likely a way to break through it – a way you didn't have before.

Additionally... you certainly don't have to do this whole songwriting thing alone. That's what the next chapter is all about.

14

THERE'S ONLY ONE WRITER'S BLOCK, BUT MANY OF YOU

"Music is powerful. As people listen to it, they can be affected. They respond."

—Ray Charles

I'll assume that by now you've already tackled writer's block just fine, but let's just say you're still struggling with even feeling *excited* about the craft. That can put a damper on how it fuels your creativity.

Working alone can be boring.

Ever notice how often music artists work together? Pharrell himself said, "You don't have to be the one with all the answers." So many songs end up having a 'featuring' bit on it as that extra flavor, beefing up excitement, passion, and praise for the art form that is songwriting. Collaborations are nitro boosters for the music industry.

After all, what's better than one brain? Two brains. And I do *love* collaborating with other songwriters and producers.

Before you collaborate with other artists, though, understand your strengths.

You'll need to assess yourself in these areas just to know where you should focus on, and where your partner(s) should then also focus on:

- Beats
- Chord progression
- Editing
- Hooks
- Lyrics
- Melody
- Riffs
- Rhythm
- Samples
- Toplining
- Overview
- A combination
- Or all the above!

You undoubtedly want a collab to work well and not be a calamity fraught with friction. So ensure whatever writing team you put yourself in, make sure it's balanced. There has to be chemistry. A synergy. The entire team you're a part of should work as a cohesive unit. If not, be prepared for a big mess as some bands end up being.

You may, of course, not want to be officially part of a production team like The Neptunes or The Smeezingtons, per se. But you'll certainly want to work with one and expand your knowledge of the craft by putting some heads together. Be *open*. Be *communicative*. Be *flexible*.

Sessions might go long. Sessions might be short. That's okay.

Be adaptive to the needs of those you're collaborating with, and make sure it's understood that those you're collaborating with return the favor.

Above all else, though, don't be a people pleaser. Honesty, as tough as it may be, in the long run it will benefit you. Sure, it may lead to conflict if you point out something that just isn't quite working in the songwriting process, but you can't avoid it. Be confident in what you bring to the table.

Avoiding conflict means you'll never get off that island, because you're afraid of getting on the boat. So get on the boat. You'll be knocked around some, but the end goal is that you're off the island, and you're heading for the mainland where all the goods are, working together to make great music and bring it all together.

Of course, find a common ground or the conflict may never resolve! But let there be a give-and-take with the relationship. You'll want a writing partner who won't be afraid to challenge you. With challenge comes inspiration, motivation, and *maybe* a little annoyance, but the tradeoff is more than profitable in your case.

Yet, be sure to find a partner that will closely harmonize with your goals.

Don't just 'settle' by any means. So put yourself out there in the songwriting community as interested in a collaboration, positioning yourself as providing *value* in the talent and wisdom you have. In other words, don't make the collaboration about *you* – even though initially that's the reason for it. Make the collab about what *you* can *contribute.*

Collabs are fun in that you often don't know where it's going to take you or your partner(s).

Pharrell once made a point on how the music industry landscape has changed dramatically: "When we're in the studio, it's fifteen people working on a song. It's just different." He went on to say that there's no longer that business pressure of you having to walk into a room like this is Shark Tank or like you got it all together.

You don't. You can come as you are, finding the right team to make it happen.

Make sure you prioritize harmony as a driving force toward success. Maintain the level of synergy you initially have with your partners throughout the course of the journey, plain and simple.

It then becomes a staple that you must agree to divide up credit in finishing a song. This can be tricky, because sometimes we often feel like *I* wrote the song and only *me*. Sadly, it wasn't just *me*. It was also my partner, or partners, and you have to recognize that.

It's common to write down on paper who did what. Whether it was producing, writing, arranging, singing, whatever. This allows an equitable and technically *legal* share of the contribution.

Lastly, never discount the power of networking.

This goes without saying in the artistic fields. Painters, novelists, actors, even lawyers – they all *network*. They learn from each other constantly – as Pharrell would say, "Recognize what you're not good at and take the other's help." It nurtures the industry. The same goes for singers and songwriters.

You can put yourself out there traditionally in many ways, such as YouTube, Instagram, TikTok, Twitch, or SoundBetter, but what about upping the odds and investing in more high-powered resources?

- Try open mics
- Compete in songwriting contests
- Join musicians' organizations
- Attend writer camps
- Participate in seminars
- Visit workshops, conferences, and symposiums

The possibilities are, in fact, quite endless. You have the world at your fingertips as a budding songwriter, so the bottom line is you're *not* alone – even if you're the only one sitting in your garage with your voice only, a pad and pen, and your mind filled with ideas.

Once again, Pharrell said it best: "Work with other people who are amazing and who can help you up your game."

FINAL WORDS

"Music is the tool to express life – and all that makes a difference."

—Herbie Hancock

If you're at this point now, you're probably only staring off into the horizon with the tools you need, the passion you have, and the will you've always wanted to become the songwriter and artist you've always dreamed of being. If that's the case, there's nothing left to say. You have all the power in the world to create your *own* tools to suit your style, and there's no right or wrong here with the flexible guidance provided.

I could, however, keep listing them over and over and over again...

- Don't just *do* songwriting. *Be* a songwriter instead.
- Explore music, and don't worry about 'formal education' or 'training'
- Listen to inspiration

- But don't wait for it to hit you!
- Mind the setbacks – and don't let them stop you
- Know how a song is structured
- Understand hooks
- Nurture your language with the power of rhyme and poetry
- Explore many other literary devices you may have forgotten about
- Practice. Train your ears. Exercise your brain.
- Sample. Copy. Adopt. Adapt. But above all else, *make your own.*
- *Please* stop judging yourself – or how your voice sounds
- Understand how melodies work and why
- Leverage technology, applications, platforms, and more
- Start recording
- Don't forget to break writer's block
- And put yourself out for possible collaborations!

The fact is I could keep beating the dead horse, but none of it will matter unless you close this book and start working on your own. At the very least, you'll always have this for reference, reinforcing the best practices you now have to achieve your goals as a songwriter, so if there was anything else I *should* say, it's this:

Start writing! And singing!

ACKNOWLEDGMENTS

I'd like to thank God for inspiring me and renewing my life with a new song every single day. This book would not be possible without His love for me.

To my parents for always supporting my dreams and constantly reminding me of my purpose. Their prayers keep me going.

To my friends and mentors who blessed me with their time throughout this project. You know who you are.

Also, I would like to express my endless gratitude to all the artists and songwriters I'm regularly learning from. Their work has been the foundation for everything I know about music.